A Voice from the Fringe

A Voice from the Fringe

Hope for the Spiritually Homeless

Jonathan Reynolds

Authentic

LONDON ● ATLANTA ● HYDERABAD

Copyright © 2006 Jonathan Reynolds

12 11 10 09 08 07 06   7 6 5 4 3 2 1

First published 2006 by Authentic Media
9 Holdom Avenue, Bletchley, Milton Keynes, MK1 1QR, UK
285 Lynnwood Drive, Tyrone, GA 30290, USA
OM Authentic Media, Medchal Road, Jeedimetla Village,
Secunderabad 500 055, A.P., India
www.authenticmedia.co.uk
Authentic Media is a division of Send the Light Ltd., a company
limited by guarantee (registered charity no. 270162)

British Library Cataloguing in Publication Data
A catalogue record for this book is available from the
British Library

ISBN-13 978-1-85078-715-0
ISBN-10 1-85078-715-8

Cover design by David Smart
Printed and bound in India by
OM Authentic Media, P.O. Box 2190, Secunderabad 500 003
E-mail: printing@ombooks.org

For Gabi, Natalie and Daniel

Contents

Foreword

Most churches are better at welcoming people on the front door than they are at guarding the back door, and as a result they fail to spot those who are leaving the church silently. How many Sundays would it take for you to realize a regular member of the congregation had silently 'gone missing'?

Jonathan and I attend the same church. Following a morning service eighteen months ago he thrust a bulky envelope into my hands and said, 'Read this and tell me what you think.' When I read Jonathan's manuscript, I knew it was an honest first-hand account of someone who had 'gone missing', and his story was crying out to be published.

When I am in a bookshop, pondering whether to buy the book I'm thumbing through, I eventually make my mind up when something leaps off the page and grabs my attention. I 'bought' Jonathan's manuscript when I read phrases like:

'I couldn't face the thought of going to church.'

'I had retreated to the fringes of church life.'

'I was worn down by the negative experiences of living at the edge of church life.'

'I have written this for those for whom the church doesn't work any more.'

On my travels I learn of too many Christians who are living on the fringe of the church, and with genuine pain I recall the vast numbers of people in churches I have pastored who have silently left the local church by an unguarded back door.

Lest you think this is another book by an angst-driven person who has written off the church, think again. This is the story of a Christian who had retreated to the fringes of church life, but who then discovered there was a small seed of hope buried beneath the rubble of disappointments and disillusionments of church experience, and the nurture of this seedling enabled him to pose some searching questions from the fringe.

It is a book that will be valuable to pastoral leadership because it is an insider's view of someone who struggles with the often meaningless culture of church life. It will be a book of warm encouragement for those who are living beyond the fringe but retain a heart for genuine Christian community. It is a loud warning to all who may be obsessed with what form the local church takes, rather than asking what life Jesus is asking us to live.

This is a book that says, 'Read me.'

I hope you will.

David Coffey
Member (with Jonathan) of a 'growing in grace' local church
and President of the World Baptist Alliance

Introduction

I started to write this book one Sunday morning after another heated discussion with my wife and children about why, yet again, I couldn't face the thought of going to church. I set out to explain to my family how I really felt about church and just how frustrated I was. Consequently, this began life as an angry rant against church culture and a barbed critique of the church and why I felt it had lost its relevance and appeal to me and to society.

There is something about writing things down, though, that helps clear the fog of your own emotions, and at some point I began to see that my feelings towards the church were blinding me to the more important issue of my own relationship with God. I was forced to acknowledge the obvious truth that the church is made up of people like me and it is my personal experience of God that makes the church what it is. I had failed to find God in the church, but in my preoccupation with its problems and my negative experiences of church life, I had lost sight of the search for God that had brought me to the church in the first place.

I also began to realize just how many people there are who, like me, have retreated to the fringes of church life because their attempts to follow and serve God have ended in disappointment, hurt, or spiritual and emotional exhaustion. Although there is no data to tell us just how many people there are who stand one step away from the church door, it no doubt reflects a trend that sees growing numbers of Christians outside the church community – and many giving up on their faith altogether.[1]

The number of people attending churches in the northern hemisphere decreases every year. Even though one or two denominations occasionally appear to buck this trend, it is usually short-lived and the net result is a shrinking Christian community that is a fraction of the size it was prior to the Second World War. In the UK, for example, regular church attendance has dropped from 21 per cent of the population in 1940 to just 10 per cent in 2000.[2]

For a while it was perhaps possible to explain this away as some kind of God-given refining process sorting out those who 'really are Christians' from those who just attend because of their Christian heritage and upbringing. With thousands of churches closing each year, however, there is a growing realization that the future of church-based Christianity in our so-called developed countries is under serious threat.

It is not simply that older members are dying off faster than new members are joining. Fewer and fewer people of recent generations born into the church have remained there and the church has lost its appeal in a secularized society. We are told that during the 1990s around one thousand young people in the UK left the church each week.[3] In spite of an increasing hunger in our communities for spiritual meaning, many who grew up with a Christian tradition are turning to alternative forms of spirituality, while others attempt to live out their Christian beliefs without the fellowship of the church. Even some older people who have been faithful church members since their youth are walking out or retiring to the sidelines, excluded and disillusioned by the changes being made in an attempt to make the church more attractive and palatable to society.

Evangelicals have not been immune to these developments, and many mainstream churches have witnessed a decline in their membership. Even in more lively fellowships, for young people leaving home increasingly means leaving the church as well, and there is a slow but significant haemorrhage of adults, people who just a few years ago were enthusiastic young Christians running youth groups, leading worship and full of passion for God and his church.

For once the church's preoccupation with attendance data is telling us something useful and alarm bells are ringing out their warning that the future is very uncertain. There are now numerous books and seminars suggesting innovative ways to restructure our churches, creative approaches to worship and novel methods of evangelism, all of which aim to make Christianity more relevant and appealing to contemporary culture. In spite of much activity, however, with some churches seeming to try one church growth formula after another in a futile attempt to fill their pews, there is no model as yet that has brought about sufficient sustained growth to reverse the downward trend in church membership. Vast amounts of energy and resource were committed to mission in the UK during the final decades of the twentieth century but the fruit was sparse and short-lived. Even where 'outpourings of the Spirit' have appeared to herald the next revival, there has been no lasting impact; blessings have faded and the church continues to dwindle.

What the statistics fail to capture, though, is the number of people in the church who are frustrated and disappointed but who choose to stay. They overlook the people who were once energetic Christians but who have drifted to the fringes of church life, those who are still active church members but who are becoming increasingly disillusioned by the fruitlessness of their labour and others who, because they are worn down by the pressures of life, are now passive members hovering at the edges of the church community. Statistics also miss those who are marginalized within their churches because of painful experiences that have rendered them ineffective. They fail to register the individuals who set out with a passion for God but who met with rejection at the hands of their Christian brothers and sisters, and those who have simply given up because their love and commitment has never been recognized.

If we could quantify it, this growing group of people would perhaps be a better barometer of the state and future of the church than the number of people leaving. By understanding the factors that exile people to their personal deserts at the margins of our fellowships we might gain some insight into why the church has lost its appeal. These are the sheep who, according to the statistics, are safely in the fold but who are, in reality, wandering alone on a cold and desolate hillside. They are the people who, were they to leave en masse, could shut down many of our churches altogether – but who could, if alternatively they were to find a renewed vision and energy, totally revitalize them.

I grew up in a Christian family, albeit a somewhat maverick one. Throughout my youth I was very active within the church community and at one point I even undertook theological studies with a view to some sort of 'full-time ministry'. However, like many of my generation, I have become increasingly disillusioned with what I have seen in the church over the years and disappointed with my own spiritual experience. The fiery visions and ideals I had at 20 had been smothered by a fog of frustration at 40 and I was ready to join the growing throng of ex-church members.

I wrote this book at a time when ill health had forced me to pull the emergency stop cord on my hectic lifestyle. This gave me an opportunity to look back at my dreams and expectations and confront the fact that in my Christian life not everything, in fact very little, had worked out as I had hoped. It is only when you stop that you realize just how much time has passed, how much water has irretrievably flowed under the bridge and how short life really is: too short to be struggling on in a spiritual wasteland or drifting year after year at the periphery of the church, but in practice long enough for that wasteland to become a normal and acceptable state in which many of us live. So, after my returning to the beginning on several occasions, this book has become something of a record of the things I have learnt on a personal journey of rediscovery, how my disappointment with the church, my anger and hurt have led to a close and sometimes painful examination of my own relationship with God and his people.

I have written this for those who, like me, were once full of zeal for their faith but now, disenchanted, disheartened and worn down by their negative experiences, are living at the outer edge of church life. This is a book for people who have burned themselves out trying to bring fruit to a barren church community, for those who have given up in discouragement after trying to balance a busy life with the demands of Christian culture, and for those who struggle on tenaciously in spite of their disappointment. It is also for those for whom the

church simply doesn't work any more, whose spiritual
expectations have not been met and whose enthusiasm
has waned to the point where they are questioning the
reality of their earlier experiences of God.

As I stepped back to examine my spiritual state I
found that there was still a small seed of hope. It may
have been trampled on and buried beneath the rubble of
my church experience, but it was still there. By holding
on to this hope, I have found the fringe has become a
place from where I can begin to discover God anew,
without the clutter of my religious culture and the baggage of my church background. I have found that my
spiritual desert was not a dead end but a staging post on
a journey that has allowed me to find a new depth of
experience with God – and even a new love for his
church. I still have a long way to go on this journey and
I frequently find myself in uncharted waters, so the book
isn't a route map or a list of shortcuts to a rejuvenated
spiritual life. Everybody's road will be different anyway.
However, in sharing some of my thoughts and experiences my aim is to encourage those on a similar road to
search out the small seed of hope in their own lives and
to discover God's gentle invitation to take the first
onward step on their personal journey with him.

The book is also a message from the fringe to encourage church leaders: leaders who are trying to understand
why some of their members are throwing in the towel,
and leaders who have themselves been worn down or
marginalized because of their attempts to swim against
the tide of their congregation or tradition. There are many
theories to explain why my generation and those since are
losing interest in the church or are no longer attracted to
it. Although many of these ideas have a great deal of
merit, this is a call to look beyond the theory and examine
the hearts of the sheep who are giving up on life in the

fold. It is a plea for leaders to recognize that although image and presentation are important, what we need is a genuine experience of God – a spirituality that makes a difference to our lives: not more entertainment. When those at the margins of our churches are brought into the warmth of a renewed relationship with God and his people, the love and life of the church will reach beyond the door to those in our communities and at the margins of society.

Jonathan Reynolds, March 2006

Notes

1. 2001 Civil Census data showed that only 10 per cent of those who consider themselves Christians attend church.
2. Peter Brierley, *Religious Trends 2000/2001*, Christian Research.
3. The English Church Attendance Survey of 1998 (Christian Research) found that about one thousand children aged under 15 left the church each week in the 1990s.

1

Reality or reverie?

Remember those earlier days after you had received the light . . .
Hebrews 10:32a

I became a Christian during the 1970s. This was a time
when many churches seemed to undergo something of a
renaissance in the way they worshipped God and prac-
tised their faith. There was a new spiritual openness,
and many congregations had been influenced by the
charismatic renewal movement that had been sweeping
the country. I found myself part of a powerful Christian
youth culture that brought a buzz of excitement and
anticipation to older church traditions.

For many Christians this was an exciting and heady
period in their lives that they now look back to nostalgically. Most of us were still very young but we had a
strong spiritual hunger to know more of God, and our
fellowship was often characterized by new depths of
love for each other. We believed firmly in a faith based
on a genuine encounter with God through his Holy
Spirit and this impacted the way we lived.

We were a generation of young Christians that
brought a renewed awareness of social justice to the

church and a vision that through our faith we could make a real difference. We were concerned about poverty and oppression; it mattered what politicians were doing to our society and we were firm in our belief that the message of Christ had something to offer our hurting world. Many of us got involved in the nationwide missions of the 1980s; we joined demonstrations against unjust regimes and initiated community projects. There was a new wave of Christian music, contemporary models for expressing our spirituality, and a fresh desire to spread the message of love and hope in a way that was relevant to our local communities.

Perhaps some of it was a bit naïve, and occasionally I cringe when I look back, but I believe our hearts were in the right place: we were happy, we had a strong sense of purpose, we 'had a life'. We were passionate about what we believed and nobody could have called us half-hearted. But what became of all our activity– More importantly, what became of those of us who were part of it? Did we disappear into evangelical indifference the day they freed Nelson Mandela? Did our zeal for love and justice become lukewarm when the Cold War ended?

In spite of our tremendous enthusiasm, we didn't set the world ablaze after all. With time the fires in our Christian communities cooled to little more than smouldering embers and the church we thought we could revolutionize is now more marginalized than ever. Some of my generation have, I am sure, gone on to develop successful ministries. Many more, however, have left the church altogether, and most of us are wrapped up in our busy lives: church is just another part of a demanding week's routine, with God somewhere towards the bottom of our long to-do lists. We believed we could change the world, but the evidence suggests that it might in fact have been the world that changed us.

What went wrong? We thought we were different, we hoped that through us God would re-establish the church as a light in our society with the same power that it had had in New Testament times – but it didn't happen. Perhaps it was all just a normal phase that every new generation of Christians goes through. Maybe it was just youthful idealism and we have simply grown up and moved on to more important things. We have different priorities now, families to support, mortgages to pay, bosses to please and lifestyles to maintain. We can't afford to rock the boat any more.

When I first became a Christian I was excited by the sense that this was just the beginning of my adventure – that I had embarked on a journey that would lead me to discover new depths to my relationship with God. I was hungry to know the God of the Old and New Testaments and I sought earnestly to find his purpose for my life. It was this healthy hunger and earnest seeking for something more of God that led me to become involved in busy church programmes and kept me heavily engaged in Christian activity for many years.

I had people around me who claimed a wealth of spiritual experiences. They declared that they knew God personally, that they had witnessed miracles and they were able to hear his voice. For a long time those who made such professions were my role models because they appeared to have the things that I believed would make my experience of God real: the things that would wipe away any doubts and make the difference to my life that I had been looking for. For a while I thought I was making progress. I believed I felt God's presence in my life and at times I tasted a peace and an awareness of God's love that seemed almost tangible. I had spiritual experiences that made me more secure in my faith, but actually knowing God seemed to remain just beyond my reach. Throughout the early years of my spiritual journey this personal relationship with God that fellow Christians spoke about so much was the thing I wanted most. But it remained elusive, like a horizon that moved further away the nearer I tried to get, and I slowly began to lose faith in those people I had regarded as examples.

Eventually, feelings of uncertainty crept in and questioning became discouragement. In an age when pastors, preachers and politicians all claim to hear and heed God's voice, this discouragement turned slowly to cynicism. And when I voiced my cynicism I was amazed to find other Christians who were also coming to terms with the fact that we seemed to have taken it all a bit too literally. In fact, one of my lasting impressions of the time I spent as a theology student is the cynicism that frequently became the basis of friendships. We felt let down, even misled, by the church and the Christians that we had once looked up to.

At some point I simply stopped thinking about it at all and accepted that the belief I had subscribed to wasn't quite what its loudest proponents claimed. Like most of my evangelical friends I still spoke about my 'personal relationship with God', and as long as I never challenged what we really meant by the terms 'personal' or 'relationship', everything looked fine. My hunger to know God became lost in the tacit acceptance that I knew him as well as one can and I buried my questions in the routines of church life.

The journey I embarked on as a young person, with a childlike hope and understanding of spirituality, had not lived up to my expectations. But somehow, subconsciously, I had come to terms with this, and the youthful experiences I had believed were from God became little more than faded memories. The personal relationship with God that I had been promised, that I had expected and searched for, hadn't really happened. By this time, though, I was so integrated and engaged in church life that it was no longer an issue, and I hadn't even noticed it was missing. It had ceased to command any serious thought because it appeared that the level of 'relationship' that I had was the accepted norm.

Gradually disappointment and disillusionment began to set in. This was perhaps precipitated by the unloving and hurtful behaviour I witnessed and experienced from Christians I had to some degree regarded as leaders and mentors, but it would be an over-simplification to attribute it entirely to that. It was just part of a growing feeling that for me, church didn't do what it said on the label and God didn't do what the church claimed he did. I had looked for a genuine difference between the church and the world, for a love, a joy and a knowledge of God that made Christians stand out in the crowd, but what I had found, in practice, bore very little resemblance to this. When you scratched beneath the thin covering of Christian culture it was not so different from the world outside the church at all. It wasn't that I expected Christians to be immune to the problems and temptations of the world or to the challenges of relationships, but I had expected something more than pat answers to my questions and I had hoped for genuine intimacy between Christians that went deeper than the superficial love I encountered.

Slowly my interest in spiritual things waned and church became little more than a necessary duty to keep the family happy. Anger was added to my cynicism as my questioning was met with rejection, and over a period of several years I drifted from being a highly motivated candidate for church leadership into the growing ranks of demoralized and disillusioned Christians bobbing, almost contentedly, amongst other flotsam and jetsam at the periphery of church life. Not quite washed up on the crowded beach of ex-church members, but a long way from the main current. It was a state that had crept up on me, a process that had gone on subtly for many years before I noticed it.

Church had formed a very important part of my childhood and, as is frequently the case with people who grow up in Christian families, I found it hard as I questioned things later in life to differentiate between upbringing, habit and genuine spiritual experience. As disenchantment took over, it wasn't so much that I stopped believing in God, I had just lost faith in the claims of my Christian background and could no longer really equate God with church life. Like other disenchanted Christians that I have known and even counselled over the years, I reached the point where I didn't have the courage to leave, but nor did I particularly see much reason for staying.

My father was a church minister and the negative and destructive sides of church life that I had observed from an early age no doubt influenced the way I viewed things as an adult. Even as a child I had never really been able to come to terms with the gulf I found between the promises I read in the Bible and the reality of life in the church, and this had fuelled my frustration as I got older. Although I could just about accept that God would want to know me, by the time I had reached middle age I no longer expected my relationship with him to be enhanced by my experience in church. For me, church had become little more than a busy institution full of mainly well-meaning people. It had not turned out to be a place where I could encounter God, and instead of the haven of love and warmth I had hoped for it was frequently a place of hurt and rejection.

I first became aware of the true extent of the desert that was taking hold of my soul a couple of years ago. I was travelling on a six-hour train journey from Düsseldorf to Munich, shut in a small compartment with a friend who was a scientist and atheist. Our long conversation turned quickly to God and the universe and I found myself forced to confront my own spiritual state. My friend was able to challenge much of what I had to say about God simply because he could see that I was questioning it myself, because so much of what I had accepted as being from God was merely the Christian culture I had unquestioningly adopted – a culture that had in many ways fallen apart for me.

The thin thread of belief that was left, I had to admit, seemed to be based largely on my fear of there being no God and the fact that I had insufficient courage to abandon the faith I had grown up with. For him it would have been a leap of faith in the dark to move to a position of belief; for me the roles were reversed and I was holding on to something that would have required a leap into the dark for me to let go of it. The difference between us was that he had a far larger chasm to cross to adopt a religious worldview than I had to abandon mine. Beneath the multiple layers of my Christian upbringing there was very little to show for the personal relationship with God I had been told was part of the Christian life.

I had been forced into an honesty that left me feeling exposed and naked before my non-believing colleague. The more I thought about it afterwards, though, the more I realized that it wasn't that straightforward – it wasn't something I could write off that easily. Although much of what I had believed to be important had become lost in the habits of church life and the clutter I had accumulated on the way to reaching middle age, it had once been very real to me. It had been more than a passing phase that I had grown out of. I realized that if I were to deny the reality of some of my early experiences of God I would be deceiving myself just as much as if I were to maintain that I really knew God personally.

I had become convinced that much of what the church claimed to offer resulted from a cultural veneer, and was in some extreme cases an outright sham, but there was a germ of faith inside me that had taken root as a result of something genuine. My experience of God was sufficiently real for me to be unable to explain it away or shake it off. It was not easy to define, nor did it allow me to claim that 'God is like this' or 'God is like that', or 'I can hear God's voice', but it was nonetheless undeniably real to me. My religious experience had perhaps been like a brief glimpse of somebody very beautiful whom you know you would fall in love with if you could only meet them, and it had left a soft and almost pleasant aching in my heart. Beneath all my doubts and disillusionment I found I still had the same gentle yearning to know God that had motivated me as a young person.

As a young Christian I had expected my beliefs to impact every fibre of my life and I had hoped for a personal encounter with a loving God that would change my very being. In practice, though, I had tried to fill the God-shaped hole that Christians so often refer to with church-shaped culture. Consequently, the spiritual journey I thought I was embarking on had become little more than a fruitless run round the block. Behind the background noise of a busy life and the voice of frustration and disappointment with the church, there was a hunger and emptiness, and the God-shaped hole was as real and as vacant as ever. It was a hole that for years I had been too wrapped up in my church life to even notice, and that in more recent times I had been unable to see because of the cataract of disillusionment and anger that had clouded my vision.

As I have shared my feelings with people from a similar background to my own I have been astonished at the number who, like me, have retired to the margins because, in one way or another, church has not lived up to their expectations. If, however, we stop and ask ourselves honestly whether all our initial enthusiasm was simply misguided idealism or if there was really something to it, we must be prepared for the consequences of the answer. If it was all youthful folly, there is no point in maintaining a façade of half-hearted religion. Most of us will find, however, that if we ignore the rhetoric of Christian culture and the voice of our own disenchantment and look truthfully at our hearts, we still have a need and desire to know God. We must acknowledge that somewhere during our journey we have lost something very precious and essential from our lives.

If we take the time to think about it, even if we take into account the veil of nostalgia that beyond a certain age seems to hang over our past, most of us must admit that we were genuinely happier in those days and we felt better about ourselves and each other. Perhaps we didn't have the same material 'quality of life', but we felt truly alive and our daily experience was richer and more focused.

Part of the problem is that we don't have the time to question any more. We are increasingly losing true control over our lives to our busy secular and church programmes, with the result that we can live at the margins of our fellowships for many years, possibly not even noticing it until we are forced to stop by something untoward. When we do stop long enough for the questions to bubble up to the surface, we find that the spiritual hunger and the joy we once knew have been replaced, at least in part, by a niggling discontentedness, by a subtle but disturbing emptiness – even by hurt and anger.

We must allow our questions to form and let them challenge what we have accepted as the normal state of our Christian lives. A frank look at both the dwindling church and the diminishing role of God in our individual lives will tell us that something is very wrong. Christian leaders acknowledge that the light of the church is rapidly disappearing below the horizon of secular society and it is no longer the place people turn to when they search for God or for spiritual sanctuary. For many of us still in the church, it would be true to say that our lives have lost the flavour they once had and the light we once sought has also been lost below our personal horizons.

If the Jesus we said we would follow really is God, we need to find out why the personal relationship with him that we had hoped for, the intimacy that we once tasted briefly when we felt the touch of his hand on our hearts, has become little more than a forgotten dream and a tired Christian cliché. If God really is the God of love, we need to understand why we didn't find the love we had expected in the church and why the love in our own lives has been replaced by disappointment, hurt and anger. If God really is the God we once believed in so strongly, we cannot carry on with business as usual, nor can we use the behaviour of our churches as an excuse for the state of our hearts. We may find ourselves on the periphery of church life, but if we truly can know God, finding him has got to be central to our lives.

> . . . *let us throw off everything that hinders and the sin that so easily entangles, and let us run with perseverance the race marked out for us. Let us fix our eyes on Jesus, the author and perfecter of our faith . . .*
>
> Hebrews 12:1-2

Beyond the fringe

For a number of years I needed to take very strong medication in order to live a near-normal life. Over time I became tolerant of the drugs and had to increase my dosage to the point where it was debatable whether the side effects were actually less pleasant than the condition the drugs were supposed to treat. The whole family suffered as a consequence but we gradually adjusted and redefined 'normal life'. I thought I had hit rock bottom when I eventually could no longer work five days a week, but I decided to try to use my new-found free time to manage my medication better.

It had occurred to me that I was taking so many tablets that I was unlikely to recognize if my health had improved, and ironically, when I tried to reduce them, the effects of withdrawal were similar to my original symptoms. I decided therefore that the only way to really assess my condition was a period totally free of medication. The withdrawal process was a nightmare but I emerged with significantly improved health that could be managed largely with over-the-counter drugs. It was quite amazing. I felt like a new person and neither I nor my family could believe the change. We couldn't understand how we had come to accept as normal the chemically induced cocoon in which I lived. In spite of this there were occasionally times when I would yearn for the foggy pain-free haze in which I had spent the last few years and the strange, numb sense of security created by the drug-induced existence that had for so long been 'normal' daily life.

In our Christian lives we very quickly define 'normal' according to our experience and learn to live with pain, disappointment and spiritual poverty – it becomes part of 'normal' church life. It is pointless suffering, though, even if its normality appears to offer our lives a certain security and continuity. When we find ourselves at the fringe, spiritually it may feel like rock bottom but it is an opportunity to encounter the rock of ages. It is a chance to break free from the things that impede our spiritual journey and an opportunity to discover God beyond our church culture and our religious backgrounds.

A popular German expression states that once your reputation is ruined you can begin to live a carefree and easy life. For many of us, this is the point we have to reach if we are to move forward, because the negative baggage we collect over the years in the church can become a ball and chain that hampers any attempt to find God. It wasn't until I was ready to walk out – when it no longer worried me what people thought if I didn't attend church or take part in Christian activity – that I began to realize that I hadn't reached the end of my spiritual journey at all, I had simply been waylaid. I had failed to find the things I was looking for but it was not because they didn't exist; I had simply accepted my drab Christian existence as normal and stopped looking.

When we have lived this way for years, resuming our journey is difficult. We become preoccupied with our negative experiences; we fill our lives with things that take our eyes off God and we hold on to the hurts and disappointment, the doubts and fears that justify our existence at the fringe. Stepping out involves the risk of further disappointment or hurt, it means letting go of the things that hinder our search for God, and it often requires a battle against a mind that craves the safety of lifeless normality. It means turning our backs on our bad experiences, no longer using the church, the behaviour of other Christians or the pressures of life as an excuse for our spiritual inertia. In practical terms it is about opening up an honest dialogue with God – about spending time alone, seeking him with an open heart and mind and allowing him to speak into our lives. It involves us honestly confronting our own questions and allowing them to challenge the assumptions and clichés that we have acquired en route – without giving in to the fear of other people's reactions or opinions but looking actively to God for answers. As we do, he will start to strip away the layers of our personal church history that have prevented us knowing him and begin to reveal himself to us in a new way.

There is life beyond the fringe – but to find it we must look beyond our churches, beyond our disappointments and hurts, and begin again to seek God.

To the point

- Do you look back nostalgically to a time when you experienced greater intimacy with God and his people?
- What were the hopes and dreams you had as a young Christian?
- Do these hopes and dreams remain unfulfilled?
- Have you allowed your hurts, disappointments, cynicism and anger to distract you from your search for God?
- What do you believe to be the things that have most hindered your walk with God?
- When did you last take time out to meditate on spiritual issues?
- Do you have a growing sense of discontentment with your experience of church life? Could this be the voice of your spiritual hunger prompting you to look beyond your church experience and seek God again?

Meditation

The parable of the lost son

Jesus continued: "There was a man who had two sons. The younger one said to his father, 'Father, give me my share of the estate.' So he divided his property between them.

"Not long after that, the younger son got together all he had, set off for a distant country and there squandered his wealth in wild living. After he had spent everything, there was a severe famine in that whole country, and he began to be in need. So he went and hired himself out to a citizen of that country, who sent him to his fields to feed pigs. He longed to fill his stomach with the pods that the pigs were eating, but no-one gave him anything.

"When he came to his senses, he said, 'How many of my father's hired men have food to spare, and here I am starving to death! I will set out and go back to my father and say to him: Father, I have sinned against heaven and against you. I am no longer worthy to be called your son; make me like one of your hired men.' So he got up and went to his father.

"But while he was still a long way off, his father saw him and was filled with compassion for him; he ran to his son, threw his arms round him and kissed him.

"The son said to him, 'Father, I have sinned against heaven and against you. I am no longer worthy to be called your son.'

"But the father said to his servants, 'Quick! Bring the best robe and put it on him. Put a ring on his finger and sandals on his feet. Bring the fattened calf and kill it. Let's have a feast and celebrate. For this son of mine was dead and is alive again; he was lost and is found.' So they began to celebrate."

Luke 15:11-24

- The son had access to all the riches he needed as long as he was with the father – it was clearly a profitable estate and there was no question about what share of it belonged to him. It was only when he tried to enjoy those riches outside a relationship with his father that he found himself in poverty. When we read this parable we tend to think of a wayward believer returning to the fold of the church, but is there a message also for those who try to find and enjoy God's blessings outside a true relationship with him – or for those who seek the blessings more than they seek the relationship?

- Although we see a young man starving and in tatters after living a wild life of wine, women and song, it is easy to forget that he had started off with a lot of money and it wouldn't have disappeared overnight. For a long time he probably didn't think of his father, and when he did he may have been able to convince himself that he had been in the right, or even that his relationship with his father was actually intact. When we are not confronted directly with something, we are masters of putting it out of our minds and even convincing ourselves that things are well when they are not. Have we lived too comfortably for too long in the belief that all is well whilst squandering the spiritual heritage God gave each of us individually when we became Christians? Are we honest with ourselves and each other about the relationship we claim to have with the Father?
- Think of a slightly different scenario. This time the son takes the money but doesn't spend it on wild living. Instead he is sensible and invests it carefully so that he has a small but secure and permanent income. His relationship with the father is just as broken as the one in the parable, but because he doesn't recognize his need for a relationship it will never be restored. Does our self-sufficiency blind us to our need of a true relationship with God?

- The attitude of the lost son was not so different to that of many young people who go through a phase when they acknowledge their parents' responsibility towards them but fail to recognize that they too have a role to play in the relationship. When we were new Christians our relationship with God was important to us, but have we become like spoilt teenagers who, though they see their parents as responsible for supplying their every need, don't actually have a maturing relationship with them? Is our relationship with God a disappointment because we have not learned to love as adults?

- The riches of the church's long Christian heritage are running out. Perhaps we don't yet recognize the famine all around us, but if the church is to have a future at the heart of society rather than at the margins, we need to seek out the Father individually as well as corporately and make our relationship with him absolutely central to our lives once again.

- At the heart of the story is the love of a father who never gives up on his children, and the message that when we do acknowledge our broken relationship there is always a way back.

> *"Even now," declares the Lord, "return to me with all your heart, with fasting and weeping and mourning." Rend your heart and not your garments. Return to the Lord your God, for he is gracious and compassionate, slow to anger and abounding in love, and he relents from sending calamity.*
>
> Joel 2:12-13

> *A remnant will return, a remnant of Jacob will return to the Mighty God. Though your people, O Israel, be like the sand by the sea, only a remnant will return.*
>
> Isaiah 10:21-22a

Prayer

Father God, I confess that I don't know you in the way I have sometimes claimed to. I come to you with my doubts and fears, my anger and my hurts, and ask that you will lead me down the path that brings me into your arms and into a genuine relationship with you. Amen.

2

The emperor's new clothes

The man who thinks he knows something does not yet know as he ought to know.

1 Corinthians 8:2

On a business trip to Israel some years ago I had the opportunity to take a journey out into the Judean wilderness. From the comfort of an air-conditioned coach our tour guide pointed out the areas where David is believed to have hidden when he was fleeing from King Saul. The landscape had a barren and serene beauty, and it was easy to imagine David meditating on his Lord and spending his time there writing psalms. It was only when we got out of the coach at En Gedi that the searing heat of the midday sun hit us, and with it the realization of the terrible conditions under which David must have lived as an outcast of the king.

One of the reasons why we stay at the fringe for so long rather than leaving our churches altogether is because it can be spiritually quite comfortable, especially if we retain just enough involvement to feel and appear committed. We are spiritually fed and watered, we come to terms with our disappointment by lowering our expectations and we stay sufficiently distant from things to avoid them affecting us too deeply. We can even continue to be part of church activity and yet be spiritually at the fringe because the pressures and responsibilities of church life prevent us hearing the parched voice of our soul. As long as we turn up for church on Sunday everyone thinks we are fine, and sometimes we even believe it ourselves. We would no doubt be surprised if we knew just how many people there are whose original enthusiasm and hunger for God has cooled and who are dangerously unaware of their spiritual dehydration because of the artificial shade and bottled water of church life.

Church can easily become like my comfortable air-conditioned coach in the middle of the desert. It can shield us from the very challenges we need for a deeper experience of God, and can even become an alternative to the refreshing spiritual oasis to which God desires to lead us. As I acknowledged the shambles of my own beliefs, I effectively stepped out of the comfort and shelter of the church. I began to question many of the accepted practices of church culture and ask how much of it really had anything to do with God. It is difficult to openly challenge the words and expressions that are deeply embedded in our evangelical vocabulary and it makes people feel very uncomfortable when we do. When I did start to question, I recognized that many of the things I had considered important in my church life had actually been a surrogate for a genuine experience of God.

When I examined the church culture I had grown up in, I found myself particularly troubled by the way many Christians talk so glibly of a personal relationship with God. I had long struggled to equate the vastness of God with the warm and cuddly way I felt he was so often portrayed by the church, and part of me wondered if it was at all possible to know him intimately. However, instead of trying to resolve the dilemma through searching for him, I found in God's mystery and magnitude a convenient way of explaining why I could talk of a 'personal relationship with God' that in fact bore no resemblance to anything else I would consider a relationship. As I looked at my own relationship with God, two very obvious things occurred to me:

1. If God is real, and if we truly can have a genuine, loving, personal relationship with him, then we must. If we can know him, this has to be our very highest priority in life. An intellectual awareness or experience of God's love for us, and even the warm fuzzy feeling we sometimes get during worship, is not a relationship – nor is it necessarily evidence of a relationship. It can, however, become a substitute for a relationship.
2. If God is, as he describes himself, love, this gives us something that we can grasp, something that is both human and divine.[1] Although it is a poor reflection, our own love gives us insight into God's nature and provides us with a benchmark against which we can assess the genuineness of our relationship with him. To honestly examine our relationship with God, we must not intellectualize his love for us or our love for him and turn it into something less than human love. God's love can only be more pure, more perfect, more intense and more personal than our human love. Therefore the relationship we are seeking with God must be more pure, more intense and just as real to us as our human relationships.

On this basis I found my own relationship with God had, in reality, very little substance to back it up, even though it was something I had simply and unquestioningly taken for granted for many years. As Christians we talk a lot about our love for God and our relationship with him, but to me as an observer from the fringe it seemed that the special Christian love I had come to equate with church life was in practice only different in that it was a diminutive kind of love. When I compared it, for example, with the imperfect human love I felt for my children or the level of communion I shared with my wife, although I would never before have admitted it, these were far more real to me than my relationship with God. I could claim to know God personally, even feel a wave of emotion at times in church, but it was something I found I was trying to convince myself of rather than a fact that I could not deny. If our love for God is less than our human love, our relationship must be less than personal.

When I was in my late twenties I moved to Bavaria. This is a beautiful part of southern Germany with mountains and lakes, lots of sunshine in summer and plenty of snow in winter. I was overwhelmed by the countryside, the picturesque towns and villages, and the sense of tradition and history that influenced cuisine, dress, music and lifestyle. Because of its strong identity it was a culture that to some degree I envied.

Generally speaking, the Bavarians are a welcoming folk and I fitted in very quickly. It didn't take me long to get used to their way of life, and the good food and the beer gardens made sure that I rapidly developed a traditional Bavarian physique. I soon learnt the language, and people occasionally mistook me for a local – on one occasion I was even persuaded to wear Lederhosen. I looked like a Bavarian, almost spoke like a Bavarian, was accepted by my neighbours as a Bavarian and at times even felt like a Bavarian – but I knew there was no way I could ever really be a Bavarian. I had simply and largely unwittingly assimilated the culture.

I found a similar situation in my spiritual life. I had acquired all the things I needed to make me feel as if I knew God, to make me look and sound as if I knew God – but the church culture I had adopted could never actually make me know him. Is it possible that one of the biggest barriers we face to actually forming a genuine relationship with God is a Christian culture that leads us to the conviction that we already know him: the belief that a deep and intimate relationship is an almost automatic consequence of our conversion?

When we become Christians it is a joyful event and we are welcomed enthusiastically into the family of the church. There are many pleasant new experiences and we find a host of new friends. As newcomers we may undergo some sort of familiarization programme to introduce us to the basic teachings and practices of the church and this, together with our rapid involvement in church activity, allows us to quickly learn the language and culture of our new community. This process of integration is extremely important, increasingly so in our secular society. However, there is often a very subtle, almost subliminal, message that communicates to the individual that they have arrived, that they now know God, as if this is a one-off process rather than the beginning of a journey that salvation has made possible. Our daily experience of church quickly fills our lives and, although we learn a great deal about God, the hunger that brought us to him in the first place is stilled by a programme of church activity. This can easily become a sort of spoon-fed spiritual fast food that suppresses our appetite for real spiritual food and our hunger for a genuine relationship with God.

Similarly, those of us who grew up in a Christian home reach a point where, if we haven't drifted away completely, we find some sort of experience of God for ourselves that establishes our own faith, independent of that of our parents. Often, though, as soon as we have got over our teenage rebellion we are drawn into the flow of church life and that minute mustard seed of a relationship with God that should have grown into a fine tree is rapidly dwarfed by the shadow of our bond to the church. We come with a sincere desire to know Christ but we are absorbed into a powerful tradition and culture that can easily and subtly relegate the desire to know God to second place behind a personal relationship with the church.

Before God we stand as individuals, but our church culture very quickly leads us down a road that promotes the development of, and dependence on, a corporate faith. We speak of intimacy with God but our experience of him is mainly in a group setting. We seek, for example, our blessing and spiritual experience within the context of church-based worship. Although this is not in itself wrong, our fellowship will only be fruitful when it is made alive by our private relationship with God. Instead, we use fellowship as a substitute for that private relationship. We know the theory but in practice the vast majority of our religious experience is in the context of church rather than on our own as individuals before God. The occasions when we do feel the warmth and closeness of God are usually against a background of group celebration, and this cannot be the sole diet we rely on to build and strengthen our faith.

In a church that constantly talks of its relationship with God and its love for each other, we adopt these words and expressions as our own, and use them without ever allowing their meaning to challenge us. We get so preoccupied with practising church and enjoying the family of our Christian community that we don't notice that the initial acquaintance we made with God has no opportunity to grow and mature. How often have I told people that they can know God as a friend, when an examination of the way I know God bears little similarity even to the way I relate to some of my business acquaintances, let alone my friends? God is not the church, and church is not some package with God inseparably thrown in – commitment to our churches does not necessarily stem from or result in closeness to God. In church we grow in our second-hand knowledge about God, but we can only really know him if we seek him on our own – if we are to have a relationship with him at all it has to be personal.

When our faith is challenged by some sort of crisis, or on those rare occasions when we are forced to examine with honesty the fruits of our relationship with God in our lives, we must often acknowledge that things aren't quite what they were cracked up to be. We put on a brave face for a while, and the theory we have learned about God helps us drive the questioning from our minds, but when we have been attending church for years and the warm welcome is long forgotten, niggling doubts can raise their heads. When perhaps our family life is in tatters or we have failed and feel rejected by our fellow Christians, or when we have burned ourselves out trying to swell the ranks of our congregations, we find that neither what we know about God nor our personal relationship with the church can help us.

We have created a church culture that promises great things in God's name, yet it is a culture that can easily distract us from actually knowing him. If church has replaced our private experience of God as the cornerstone of our faith, it is very easy to rob him of some of his divine nature through the touchy-feely, non-offensive god that we are tempted to create to fill an emotional void. In our

hearts we may want to know the true God, but if in practice the church takes the place of God in our lives, we
diminish the great 'I Am' to something like a modern
monarch in a democratic system – with all the trappings
of power, but in reality with no authority whatsoever,
because the business of governing lies with the people.

We have unwittingly created a Christian subculture
that can provide us with a satisfying covering of spirituality and the mirage of a relationship with God. But
when we measure this relationship honestly against the
benchmark of God's love, we may find it has little in
common with what is promised or with what we had
initially hoped for when we came to Christ. These are
promises that can only be fulfilled by God and not by an
evangelical image we have created ourselves. If we have
assumed a relationship with him that in reality does not
exist, we are deceiving ourselves – and we are missing
out on the deep joy of knowing and growing in a revelation of God's love. It is no wonder that we feel let
down by our Christian experience, because instead of
knowing God we have exchanged the filthy rags of our
own righteousness for a fine suit of Christian culture – a
culture that has more in common with the 'Emperor's
new clothes' than with the wedding gown of the bride of
Christ.[2]

In the Gospel of John, Jesus talks of us being grafted
into him.[3] If instead we are grafted into the church, nothing we do or say will produce the fruits of the Holy
Spirit – the very nature of God in our lives that was
intended to flow through that graft. Our faith must be in
God, but often, though our hope may be in God – sometimes an almost desperate hope that there is in truth a
God – our faith and security are really in the church. No
matter how sincere we are, how dedicated we are to our
churches, our faith will not grow and the church will not

be the light it was meant to be unless knowing God is central to our individual lives.

This is not to imply that Christians are insincere or that they are not good people. It just means that many of us have been fooling ourselves about a relationship with God that has failed, so far, to mature. If we take the trouble to go into the world outside our churches and look at the people we meet, we will see that they really are not so different, that we Christians are not so special after all. Amongst our non-Christian friends and our work colleagues, amongst the people who make it their vocation to serve our communities, people with other faiths, even people whose behaviour we may reject as wrong, we will be shocked and challenged by how many 'good' and lovely people there are. The things that would make us stand out in the crowd – the fruits of a genuine relationship with God – are missing. We may not see the transparency of our own clothing, but secular society does – and we wonder why we are not taken seriously by nonbelievers any more. Perhaps we are still a bastion of a few moral values, but for those outside the church we are little more. Why? Because the God-shaped hole in our lives is filled with the paraphernalia of church culture and we have not truly discovered the treasure of knowing God.

As long as our definition of God's blessing is rousing worship, overflowing pews and material security we cannot genuinely experience God's blessing. But when our requests to God are driven by our heartfelt desire to know him, when the treasure we are seeking is a relationship with him, all of these other things and more will be given to us.[4] When we stop chasing blessings that toss the church through a sort of spiritual 'boom and bust', and begin to grow in maturity through intimacy with God, the salt of the church community may begin again to influence the flavour of our society.[5]

When we came to God, we found the road but not the destination; we found the field but not the treasure.[6] He gave us the church because he knew we would need fellow travellers, but he never intended it to replace an intimate relationship with the true guide, Jesus Christ. If we have looked for God in our church culture we should not be surprised if we are disappointed – because it is only when we find God in our hearts that he will be present in the church.

> *. . . I consider everything a loss compared to the surpassing greatness of knowing Christ Jesus my Lord . . .*
>
> Philippians 3:8

Beyond the fringe

It is very easy to have a false sense of well-being in the church. We can fall into the trap of developing a corporate 'relationship with God' based on our fellowship experience, and our personal relationship with the church can actually suppress our hunger to know him. When we look beyond our religious culture and weigh our relationship with God in the balance of Scripture, the chances are we will find it wanting.

If our faith is to have meaning, vitality and lasting blessing we must return to the roots of our spiritual adventure – our desire and need to know God – and lay aside the preconceived ideas and assumptions we have adopted from our church culture. We must banish all clichés from our minds and ask ourselves honestly just how personally we really know this all-powerful God, originator of all, whose magnificence, might and authority we only just glimpse in the vastness of creation. If this really is the God we worship, our journey beyond the fringe must be driven primarily by our desire to know him.

Think for a moment of the implications of God really being God. Take some time to meditate on the imagery used in the Bible to describe him and the words of the songs we sing in worship. Do we really know this God? If God is the God we claim he is, there has to be something more than our current experience of him. What do we really mean when we say that we can know God personally? Even if we judge this in terms of our earthly relationships, which in theory are only a poor reflection of the relationship we should enjoy with God, do we have the dialogue, the intimacy, the assurance of mutual love that we should? Is there the fruit in our lives that is to be expected from closeness to God? We cannot afford to take it for granted that we have a relationship with God. But at the same time, neither should the fact that we may have sought him only in the culture of the church rule out the possibility of us truly knowing him.

We live in a noisy world in which we have forgotten how to be alone with ourselves. We must find a place where we can be truly alone with God – a place where we are not distracted, where we can be silent before God and allow his presence to enter our hearts. If we are to know God we need time when we shut out the sounds of the world, our minds and even our church culture. It is only when we spend time in the quiet of this private place, in the temple of our own hearts, that we can honestly examine our relationship with God, and it is only here that the seed of relationship that God planted in our lives can grow.

If we look at the Old Testament, King David is famous for many things, but one of the most important things recorded about him is that he was a man after God's heart.[7] This could only be the case if David's relationship with God was the most important thing in his life. This was not an automatic relationship. He experienced God's love for him during the years spent alone tending his father's sheep in the wilderness and the months spent hiding from Saul in the burning heat of the desert sun. Throughout these times he was isolated from the culture of his religion. In this arid wasteland, when he had no choice but to flee to the margins of his society, he had no temple or scriptures, no priest nor the opportunity for corporate worship. He was forced to find God in the temple of his own heart, and as he did, a genuine relationship was formed that no battles, disappointments or failures could take away.

To the point

- Do you ever question what you really mean by some of the Christian words and expressions you use?
- How personal is your personal relationship with God?
- Have you allowed your relationship with the church to come between you and a relationship with God?
- How long does the joy of corporate worship stay with you after a church service?
- Do you know the lingering peace and contentment that comes from regular private worship and meditation?
- Have you allowed your negative expectations of church to lower your expectations of God?
- When did you last meditate on the nature of God?
- Have you discovered the sense of awe at the mystery and magnificence of God when you meditate on him outside the box of your church background?

Meditation

The parable of the sower

Then he told them many things in parables, saying: "A farmer went out to sow his seed. As he was scattering his seed, some fell along the path, and the birds came and ate it up. Some fell on rocky places, where it did not have much soil. It sprang up quickly, because the soil was shallow. But when the sun came up, the plants were scorched, and they withered because they had no root. Other seed fell among thorns, which grew up and choked the plants. Still other seed fell on good soil, where it produced a crop – a hundred, sixty or thirty times what was sown . . .

"Listen then to what the parable of the sower means: When anyone hears the message about the kingdom and does not understand it, the evil one comes and snatches away what was sown in his heart. This is the seed sown along the path. The one who received the seed that fell on rocky places is the man who hears the word and at once receives it with joy. But since he has no root, he lasts only a short time. When trouble or persecution comes because of the word, he quickly falls away. The one who received the seed that fell on the thorns is the man who hears the word, but the worries of this life and the deceitfulness of wealth choke it, making it unfruitful. But the one who received the seed that fell on good soil is the man who hears the word and understands it. He produces a crop, yielding a hundred, sixty or thirty times what was sown."

Matthew 13:3-8, 18-23

We often use this passage to explain why our evangelistic efforts produce so little fruit and as a source of encouragement when the words we preach fall on deaf ears. When Jesus explains the parable he puts it in the context of a spiritual battle in which those who have not completely understood the message of God's kingdom are likely to have the seed that was sown in their hearts snatched away.

He describes four different scenarios in which the seed that was planted failed to grow. It is useful to look at the parable in the context of our ability to understand God's word rather than simply in relation to evangelism and conversion. It is also helpful if we think of it in broader terms of spiritual growth and our Christian journey over many years rather than just what happens to the seed of the gospel immediately after sowing.

- The hard, infertile path is not necessarily those who reject the word; rather it can also refer to those who are unable to grasp it. This suggests two things:
  1. We may have failed to communicate the message in a way that people comprehend.
  2. Our failure to communicate in a way that is understood reflects our own inadequate understanding of the message and the lack of impact it has had on our lives.
- When we think of rocky, shallow soil, we usually associate this with the unsuitable state of a person's heart – 'Perhaps their conversion wasn't real, perhaps they didn't really want to repent.' If, however, we look at this in the context of our ability to comprehend, since when was an inability to understand a sin? If we do not have sustained spiritual growth in our lives and if we are not progressing towards spiritual maturity, have we really tried to understand what it means to know God? We will only understand, only grow, if we seek with all our hearts until we do understand. Seek and you shall find.[8] Do you lack wisdom? Ask![9] It would be a tragedy to lose what has grown in

our hearts in the face of doubt or even persecution because we haven't appreciated what knowing God really means to us. The onus is on us to put down deep and strong roots – if we do, we can thrive even in poor soil and desert conditions.

- It is clear that the worries, riches and temptation of this world can blur our understanding of God's message. However, we should note that the third plant continued to grow – its only defect was a failure to produce fruit. It is dangerous to underestimate the evil one to whom Jesus refers. He will employ his understanding of our nature to deceive us most cleverly, and if anything he is likely to use things that are inherently good and appropriate to ensnare us. We may even mistakenly believe we have growth, which makes it all the more important to take an honest look at the fruits in our life.

- The seed of God's word that is sown in the good soil of our hearts should result in roots into the heart of God. If instead we put roots down into our churches, it may be good soil but the culture and practices we have developed become like a plant pot and we very quickly become pot-bound. If we depend on the nutrients in the soil of the church and don't put a deep tap root into God we will have enough to grow and live – but only up to a point. Above ground everything looks fine when we compare ourselves with similar plants. It is only when we look closely at the Bible that we realize that our growth is stunted, that our leaves are undersized, and if there is any fruit at all it is small and fragile, and rarely ripens.

- With our roots in the soil of the church we may appear disease-free and look nice in the living room, but being bonsai believers was never part of the plan. It is only when the church is built of like-minded people, seeking to put roots down deep into God and accepting responsibility for their own relationships with God, that it can be the body and bride of Christ that Jesus had in mind: a fruitful, glorious, loving family that shines out like a light in the darkness of our society, a haven of peace and love in an increasingly fragmented, loveless and fearful world.

"I am the true vine, and my Father is the gardener. He cuts off every branch in me that bears no fruit, while every branch that does bear fruit he prunes so that it will be even more fruitful. You are already clean because of the word I have spoken to you. Remain in me, and I will remain in you. No branch can bear fruit by itself; it must remain in the vine. Neither can you bear fruit unless you remain in me.

"I am the vine; you are the branches. If a man remains in me and I in him, he will bear much fruit; apart from me you can do nothing. If anyone does not remain in me, he is like a branch that is thrown away and withers; such branches are picked up, thrown into the fire and burned. If you remain in me and my words remain in you, ask whatever you wish, and it will be given you. This is to my Father's glory, that you bear much fruit, showing yourselves to be my disciples."

John 15:1-8

Do not merely listen to the word, and so deceive yourselves. Do what it says. Anyone who listens to the word but does not do what it says is like a man who looks at his face in a mirror and, after looking at himself, goes away and immediately forgets what he looks like. But the man who looks intently into the perfect law that gives freedom, and continues to do this, not forgetting what he has heard, but doing it – he will be blessed in what he does.

James 1:22-25

Prayer

Father, show me where I have substituted the blessings and riches you have given me through your church for the reality of knowing you personally. Show me the place in my heart where I can meet and converse with you, where the seedling that you planted there long ago can grow into a strong and fruitful tree. Fill my heart, Lord, with your presence and awake a hunger in me to know you more. Amen.

Notes

[1] 1 Jn. 4:8.
[2] Rev. 19:7-8.
[3] Jn. 15:1-17.
[4] Mt. 6:33.
[5] Mt. 5:13.
[6] Mt. 13:44.
[7] 1 Sam. 13:14.
[8] Mt. 7:7-12.
[9] Jas. 1:5.

3

Unfaithful hearts

"I myself said, 'How gladly would I treat you like sons and give you a desirable land, the most beautiful inheritance of any nation.' I thought you would call me 'Father' and not turn from following me. But like a woman unfaithful to her husband, so you have been unfaithful to me, O house of Israel," declares the LORD.

Jeremiah 3:19-20

The Bible tells a love story, a tale of God's infinite love for the human race, for Israel, for his church and for each of us as individuals. It also recounts a long history of sordid affairs – a relationship in which one partner is repeatedly unfaithful and the jealous love of the other is expressed in a cycle of anger, compassion and forgiveness time and time again. Packed with the intense emotion of a spurned lover, it describes God's undying yet rarely requited love and his patience in the face of rejection. It paints a picture of a heart that is voluntarily broken and a life that is sacrificed on the altar of love to save a wayward bride. We read of Israel's turbulent relationship with God and find it hard to understand how they could be so foolish. In our minds we picture them as primitive folk running after the gods of other tribes and committing sinful and rebellious acts at every opportunity – but if we examine the roots of their behaviour, we are forced to ask ourselves if we are really so different.

Although the people of Israel had seen mighty demonstrations of God's love as he brought them out of Egypt, they could not believe he loved them enough to fulfil his promise of a homeland, and consequently they wandered aimlessly in the desert for forty years.[1] If they had grasped the vastness of God's love for them and understood what that love really meant, they would not have been ashamed that they didn't, like their neighbours, have an idol to carry into battle.[2] If they had not taken his love for granted, they might not have flirted with the gods of the surrounding nations and provoked his anger.[3] Since God's love was not real to them, they could not appreciate the value it bestowed on them, and so they lived in unfaithfulness as if they were indeed worthless, preferring dead idols and lifeless rituals to the love of a living God. Whether it was due to their inability to comprehend God's immense love for them or the way they took his love for granted, the children of Israel lived as if they were not loved.

With the benefit of hindsight we can recognize Israel's folly. We can even empathize with God's sense of rejection and point a finger at Israel's error, but would we have made the same mistakes? Has God's love for us lost its meaning and importance in our lives? Were we ever truly aware of the implications of being loved by the God of love in the first place? Are we going into life's daily battles with the acceptable idols of today whilst living in a desert we have convinced ourselves is God's kingdom? If we have substituted a relationship with the church and its culture for a relationship with God, can we honestly claim to live as if we are loved by God? If we have given up on church in disappointment, are we also in danger of giving up on a God whose love we have not yet truly tasted?

The imagery of love and marriage is used throughout the Bible to portray God's love for his people. Unlike the interactions between humans and the gods of ancient mythology, God's love is presented as being much more like our own, as something real, down to earth and full of feelings we can all relate to. It is the divine blueprint for our own love and we should not fear to see some facets of God's nature reflected in our own emotions if it helps us to understand our relationship with him. If we then consider the intensity of love we feel or once felt for our partners and our children, the sacrifices we would make on their behalf, and the pain and anger we feel when our love is rejected, the intensity of God's love, pain and anger must be an order of magnitude greater.

For the human heart there can be few experiences more distressing than love that is taken for granted, scorned and trodden underfoot. Of greater intensity than physical pain, there is little that hurts more than the rejection experienced in a one-sided relationship. The object of our love is aware only of their own needs and, oblivious to the value of our affections and blind to our commitment, never returns our love. In our world of failed relationships, we should understand now, better than ever, how God feels when his people take his love for granted – but we nevertheless quickly lose sight of his love in the hustle and bustle of our busy church and secular lives. We talk of his love but don't recognize the implications it has for the way we live. We intellectual- ize it and presume on it – and like Israel we eventually begin to live as if we are unloved by God. If we have only a theoretical knowledge of his love it may influence our minds and, to some extent, change our behaviour, but some form of unfaithfulness will be inevitable in the end.

Perhaps more tragic than a love taken for granted is a love that has never really been recognized. Our inability to see that we are loved by a partner, parent or child is the cause of much heartbreak in our society. Without certainty in love, actions are not interpreted in love's context and we become vulnerable to hurt through misunderstandings. This leads to missed intimacy and leaves a tender but unnecessary void in our hearts. When we doubt the reality of a person's love for us or our own worthiness of that love, consciously or subconsciously we will be tempted to seek our comfort elsewhere. Damaged by lifestyles and a society that erodes our self-esteem, how many of us miss out on valuable relationships because we are unable to recognize when we are truly loved? If we have never embraced the reality of God's love for us, our own love for him can never truly develop and mature. If we fail to recognize the true worth of his love, we will be unable to see the value and significance his love bestows on us. If we don't understand what we mean to him, disappointment and unfaithfulness will be unavoidable.

In our human relationships we probably won't have strings of lovers, but there are plenty of other things that compete for the space in our hearts that our first love used to occupy – and our infidelity, though sterile, is just as painful in the end. Our lives become cluttered with work, hobbies, dreams and ambitions, and even church, and if we are not careful, love evaporates imperceptibly like the morning dew. The love we had, that was once vibrant and intense, quickly and subtly dissolves into a pool of indifference. We talk but we don't communicate any more. We live in the same house and share the same bed but it is a relationship in appearance only. The seed of our passion may have grown many branches, but if it has failed to put down roots in the soil of true love and friendship, the relationship will fail. We give up on the visions and ideals we had when we fell in love and settle instead for doing the right thing, fulfilling our duty as a partner – but we are no longer lovers. The dream we had of growing old together, with maturing and deepening friendship turning the champagne of our romance into the full-bodied love of an old wine, just hasn't happened. The person is still there, but gone is the passion, the fire of desire replaced with an icy matrimony.

If we have not grasped God's love for us, our relationship with him will follow the same pattern as our human relationships. Our lives will be filled with the clutter of our church culture, our busy church programmes, or our anger, hurt and hectic secular lives as we give up on church. The dreams and visions we had as young Christians will be buried under the debris of our disappointment, and church will at times feel cold and inhospitable. We rationalize the state of our relationship with God just as we do that of our human relationships. We explain things away and although our love grows cold, we adapt, and this becomes the new status quo. Rules, regulations, society's conventions and even fear of the consequences of separation can help maintain a façade of love, but they will never replace real love either as a source of happiness or as an incentive to faithfulness. Until we realize just how precious God's love is, our spiritual hunger for his love will not be met. We can maintain a show for so long but eventually we end up nursing our wounds at the fringes of church life.

Our initial encounter with God may have been filled with an awareness of his love for us, or if we grew up with Christian parents it may have been slower, more like an arranged marriage. For most of us, at some point in the early days of our faith, there was an experience of love that we had hoped would blossom into something personal and tangible. Many of us, though, must, if we are honest, admit that our experience of God's love has largely failed to live up to our expectations. Could it be that, as with our talk of a 'personal relationship with God', we have reduced talk of God's love for us to another shallow cliché? Does the diminutive image of God we have created as part of our church culture also reduce our revelation of his love for us? Have we drifted into an intellectual assumption of God's love for us without truly taking on board the reality and the implications of being loved by an omnipotent God? If we are unable to see ourselves and each other through the loving eyes of God we have very little chance of remaining immune to the gods of this world. If our own self-esteem and the value we place on each other are not informed by God's love, it is inevitable that we will hurt and discourage each other. We may pull ourselves together and maintain the outward impression of a happy relationship with God and with the people in our church, but how much is really left of that initial sense of God's love that drew us to him in the first place?

I remember once, as a teenager, walking across a broad, open field and suddenly being overwhelmed by a sense of the vastness of the universe, with a crushing awareness of my own smallness and insignificance in the face of it. A feeling that was replaced a few seconds later by what I can only describe as a drenching with God's love – a brief glimpse of how he sees me and my value in his 'big picture' scheme of things. It was a brief encounter, a taste – and though it was euphoric, it was forgotten almost as quickly as a kiss.

In spite of experiences like this, I have been forced to admit that a great deal of my adult life has been spent living out an arid, loveless faith. In my early days I spent much of my time looking earnestly for something more of God and chasing ideals in the hope that I would find God in them. But as time moved on, I drifted further and further into a barren spiritual wilderness, because the message of the reality of God's love for me, with all its consequences, implications and responsibilities, had not progressed from my head to my heart.

Is it possible that in spite of all our songs and talk of God's immense love for us, we have forgotten, or never really learnt, what being loved by him truly means? Could it be that the concept we have of God's love for us has got as far as our intellect, but the reality of his love has not taken root in our hearts and, instead of growing, our initial revelation of his love has withered and died? We have moments when we feel as if we have seen the hem of the garment of God's love, and in these moments we are alive and full of love ourselves – but it doesn't take long for this to dissolve into indifference in the busyness of our daily lives and church routines. Are we like the Children of Israel who, in spite of all they had seen, could not get their head around the idea that God loved them enough to bring them into the Promised Land? Is this the reason why we have landed at the fringe – is this why we found the church so disappointing? If our hearts are a loveless wilderness sustained by manna from our pulpits but without the fruits of God's love, we will be unable to avoid drifting in and out of unfaithfulness. Just as the people of Israel were found wandering in the desert, we become nomads in our spiritual no-man's-land, wondering what happened to the promised blessing and revival.

I don't recall very much about my wedding day: it went by like a carousel ride. I got on in the morning, then there was a whir of faces and suddenly it was all over. The one thing that is clearly imprinted on my mind, though, is how wonderful my bride looked. I found her utterly beautiful, and I was so overwhelmed by feelings of love and warmth for her that at times I was moved to tears. Even now it sometimes affects me in the same way when I look at our wedding photographs. In that moment she was absolute perfection for me, my love far bigger than any imperfection she might have had. Although a poor human illustration, it was a brief insight into the way God's love for his church unlocks his grace and bestows beauty, perfection and holiness on the bride of Christ.

But while my wedding painted a picture of God's love, my marriage has often shown me how easily we can lose sight of the love our partner has for us and how ugly we then become. How easily, if a profound love doesn't begin to form when all that's left of the big day is the photographs, habit can take over and tacit agreements on behaviour build a functional but sterile relationship. They say that love is blind, but in reality it is love that helps us to see. Our love opens our eyes to the beauty in another, and their love helps us see the beauty and value in ourselves. If we lose sight of that love, we very quickly forget how that person regards us and how we really look – and even if we were once the perfect bride, our beauty will begin to fade when we step outside the bridegroom's love. If we are to experience again the joy and freedom, the sense of purpose we once felt as we first came to God, if we are to rediscover the beauty we once saw in his church, the knowledge of God's love for us as individuals and as a church needs to become a reality in our lives.

> "'Return, faithless Israel,' declares the LORD, 'I will frown on you no longer, for I am merciful,' declares the LORD, 'I will not

be angry for ever. Only acknowledge your guilt – you have rebelled against the LORD your God, you have scattered your favours to foreign gods under every spreading tree, and have not obeyed me,'" declares the LORD. "Return, faithless people," declares the LORD, "for I am your husband."

Jeremiah 3:12-14a

Beyond the fringe

When we read of the love God showed to Israel we cannot understand how they could have been so unfaithful to him, but if we too fail to comprehend the extent of his love we will unwittingly drift into unfaithfulness ourselves. If we don't recognize his love, if we think we are unworthy of it, or if we have intellectualized his love and taken it for granted, we will be unable to enjoy a relationship with God or with his church. We may wonder why the church and even our Christian homes can, at times, feel unfriendly and hostile: why hurts, damaged relationships and broken hearts sometimes characterize our Christian communities. But when our hearts become unfaithful, we inevitably absorb the culture of the gods of the nations around us into our lives and into the church, and the gods of self, greed, jealousy and ambition will infiltrate our families and congregations.

A friend of mine once shared with me his sense of desperation because he felt unable to build a lasting relationship with the girl he loved. The problem was that he simply could not believe that she really cared for him, or that she took his love for her seriously. His paranoia that she didn't love him caused doubts and insecurities that in turn led to conflict and hurts. Although in reality she worshipped the ground he walked on, he came close to giving up on the relationship because he could not believe in her love.

This wasn't the first time my friend had fallen in love. He had once given up everything to follow his heart but his love had been rejected. As a consequence his subconscious was telling him that he was unlovable, that there must be something fundamentally wrong with him. His low self-esteem had left him feeling unworthy of love and he was unable to see his girlfriend's affection even when it stared him in the face. He failed to recognize every gesture of love she made, and every time she didn't call or couldn't spend time with him he took it as confirmation that she didn't really care.

One of the biggest hurdles we face to knowing God's love is the image that we sometimes have of ourselves – the feeling that we are somehow unworthy of love. Even though we often have a warm and fluffy image of God in our minds, we tend to picture ourselves as unlovable, rotten sinners. This can be compounded by our human experiences of love: the hurt and rejection we encounter in our church or secular lives, the cold uncompassionate legalism of some denominations or the manipulation of over-sensitized consciences by others can leave us with negative expectations and the subconscious belief that we cannot truly be loved by God. The Bible is frank about what it regards as sin and does not gloss over the fact that there is sin in our lives. However, it also makes it clear that when God looks at us he sees the individual rather than our sin, that he looks upon us as a parent regards their child rather than as a judge regards a criminal. Christ died because he sees something in us that is precious, something so valuable that he wants to know us, something so good it is worth dying for. Of course he sees our fallen nature, but he looks beyond this to the good, the precious and the God-like that made him choose to die so that we could be free to know his love.

To move beyond the fringe, we need to learn to look at our lives from beyond the cross. When we stand in front of the cross we hang our head in shame at the evil that caused such a horrific death. From beyond the cross Christ sees in us a wonderful person, of greater value than we can ever imagine, a person on whom he wants to shower his love in practical and tangible ways. God has taken upon himself the onus to reveal his love to us through the extravagance of his creation and in more personal and individual ways as he teaches us to trust him.

If, as individuals and as a church, we are ever to experience the fruitfulness that we had hoped for when we came to Christ, if our generation of Christians is to stop dying in the desert, if the bride of Christ is to regain her beauty, we have to find a new and growing certainty of God's love for us. God's love is the motivation for our spiritual journey; it was the call of his love that caused us to set out in the first place and the sacrifice of his love that made the journey possible. As we move out of the desert into the promised land of his love we will begin to find in our lives the first fruits of a genuine revelation – our love for him.

To the point

- Are you missing out on an encounter with the God of Love, because love is no longer at the heart of your image of God?
- Do you have a growing awareness of the way God sees you, or is this something you know in theory only?
- Is your self-esteem based mainly on the opinions of others?

- Do you ever ask yourself how Christ feels about the people in your church?
- Has an unfaithful heart prevented you from tasting God's love?
- Do you ever think about the impact that being loved by God should have on your life?

Meditation

The parable of the hidden treasure and the pearl

> *"The kingdom of heaven is like treasure hidden in a field. When a man found it, he hid it again, and then in his joy went and sold all that he had and bought that field.*
>
> *"Again, the kingdom of heaven is like a merchant looking for fine pearls. When he found one of great value, he went away and sold everything he had and bought it.*
>
> Matthew 13:44-46

- There are several parables about the kingdom of heaven, all of which reveal how complex and mysterious it is. However, in a kingdom ruled by a God who is love, love must be its greatest treasure. In our world, where so much of life's pain and tragedy could be resolved through genuine love, the treasure of God's heavenly love has to be priceless.
- The treasure hunter and the pearl merchant would not have found anything if they had not been wholly committed to searching in the first place. All that was required of them was to search with all their energy. The desire to give up everything came when they found what they were looking for.
- There is a difference between searching and sacrifice. If we confuse our sacrifice of time, money, and energy

to fulfil the expectations of our churches with our personal search for God, we will not find the treasure of his love.

- We are often afraid to search for a deeper relationship with God because of what we might have to give up when we find him – but when we begin to recognize the vastness of God's love, we realize that relatively speaking we have nothing worth keeping. When we discover how priceless God's love is, and the price he paid so that we can know it, we see that we really have nothing we could give up that comes anywhere near its value.

- One of the most powerful idols in today's society is our independence. We talk of freedom and choice, of people being self-made, but the self-made person is really a selfish person. If we hold on to our independence like a valuable treasure, we will never discover the more precious gift of love and dependence.

- The kingdom of the loving God is also compared with a very small seed that becomes a huge tree, and with yeast that takes over the whole batch of dough. Our understanding of God's love is something we will grow in as we nurture the seed of his kingdom through our relationship with him. When the seed of God's love begins to grow in us, the nature of the God of love starts to take over our whole being.

It is easy to talk of God's love, but extremely hard to imagine it. It can nevertheless be a helpful exercise to find a quiet place and just meditate for a while on what it means to be loved by God. Find somewhere surrounded by signs of God's amazing power – a mountain top, a ship at night – a place where your noisy thoughts are subdued by the awesomeness of God's vast creation.

Think for a while of the people most precious to you
and the intensity of the love you feel for them. Don't try
to work anything up but, in the stillness of your heart,
ask God through his Holy Spirit to reveal to you his love
– a love that is infinitely more powerful than even the
deepest affection we feel for those we value most. God's
love for us is not just some abstract concept. He gave up
the person most precious to him in order to prove it.

We have been given an intellect, emotions and an
imagination that can help us capture a sense of God.
Although it is impossible within the confines of human
thought, we should use the faculties he has given us to
try and grasp what we can of his nature, to help underpin an awareness of God's presence in our lives. We
should allow our sense of God's greatness in the wonders of the world he has given us to point to the love that
he has for us. The God who made the universe loves us
– a fact that is more awesome than the stars.

> *"Even now," declares the Lord, "return to me with all your
> heart, with fasting and weeping and mourning."*
> *Rend your heart and not your garments. Return to the Lord
> your God, for he is gracious and compassionate, slow to anger
> and abounding in love, and he relents from sending calamity.
> Who knows? He may turn and have pity and leave behind a
> blessing . . .*
>
> Joel 2:12-14a
>
> *How long, O men, will you turn my glory into shame? How
> long will you love delusions and seek false gods?*
>
> Psalm 4:2
>
> *"For God so loved the world that he gave his one and only
> Son . . ."*
>
> John 3:16

Prayer

Lord, forgive me because I have not lived as if I am loved by you. Open my eyes to the idols in my life and help me to set them aside as I seek the treasure of knowing you. I call you Father, yet I have only just begun to grasp the extent of your love. As I come to your cross, help me to appreciate that amazing gesture of love, and as I give you my heart, show me a glimpse of how you see me. Amen.

Notes

[1] Num. 14:11, 31-33.
[2] Ex. 32:1.
[3] Ps. 78:57-58.

4

First loves

We love because he first loved us.

1 John 4:19

At some point during his late teens, my father lost his sense of smell. It didn't happen overnight. It disappeared slowly over a period of years, so that by the time it had gone completely he could no longer remember what living with the ability to detect and differentiate between aromas was like. He got used to living without it, and only when someone or something made him aware of a particular scent did he miss it. (Odours are great for triggering feelings and memories, but try to remember one!) There was only one occasion when the lack of this sense nearly made a crucial difference to his life. A couple of years ago I visited him while my mother was away, and as he opened the door to let me in I was nearly knocked down by the intense smell of gas. At some point a few hours earlier he had accidentally turned on the cooker and the house was absolutely full of gas – had the cooker remained on much longer it would only have taken a spark from an electrical appliance being switched on to cause an explosion.

It is amazing how quickly we forget the importance of things that we once considered essential, how things that used to play a central role in our life can disappear without us missing them. We may have tasted a love for God when we first came to him, but if this love has failed to take root in our hearts, our love for him, like our concept of his love for us, becomes academic – the passion we once had becomes little more than a fleeting fad. We may not even notice that it has disappeared, because we regard our love for God as an assumed constant in the formula of our Christian lives. In reality, though, it is the defining variable and if it is missing we are left with little more than dull, lifeless religion and a false sense of security in our faith.

As a young Christian I found a longing in my heart to love God and a mysterious, but nonetheless genuine, sense that in spite of the abstractness of the idea, I actually did love him. As a child I had 'given my heart to Jesus', and although as adults we might be too sophisticated to use this term in any other context than Sunday school, it is the best way I can find to express what the experience meant to me at the time. In childlike innocence, it was no less real than giving my heart – giving myself – to a lover, but just as the love for a partner often disappears without us noticing, at some point that feeling of having given my heart to God slipped through my fingers. It wasn't that I consciously took my heart back; I just seemed to have stopped thinking about it. In so doing, the fact that I had pledged to love and follow Christ drifted into the dark recesses of my subconscious, far removed from my busy, active life.

From the fringes of church, without the songs and sermons to stir my emotions, I realized that a love for God hardly featured in my life. The thing that shocked me most was just how little thought I had actually given to it over the years – that something so absolutely central to the Christian faith could, in practice, have been so peripheral to my life for the best part of two decades. Loving God was part of my vocabulary, but it had not truly penetrated the substance of my life, my thoughts and my actions. In the same way that I had acquired the term 'a personal relationship with God' without dwelling much on its meaning, I would talk freely of my love for God without ever asking myself if it were true. My love was dry and intellectual, and it couldn't have been further removed from the love that God, through his word and through his own love, requires of us.

The renewal movements of the sixties and seventies generated a new hunger for intimacy with God and a desire to see the church transformed and functioning as a beacon of love in our society. Like King Josiah, we sought to bring restoration to the temple.[1] We too felt as if we had rediscovered the law – not the old law but the New Covenant, the covenant of Jesus through which our relationship with God was based entirely on grace through faith. With this fresh revelation of God's grace we discovered a new freedom and joy in our worship. It was a season of love and grace that brought with it a natural desire to please God and to clear out anything unholy from the temple of our lives. Like a child responding to a parent's affection, we could not help but return love for the love of God we had tasted.

The legacy of the renewal movement did not produce the lasting revival some predicted, however, and none of the more recent movements that were proclaimed as outpourings of the Spirit has led to a significant and sustained reversal of the church's decline. Could it be that when we discovered grace, we did not take on board the law of love on which the New Covenant is based, that we did not recognize that although grace is free, it requires the response of a loving heart? We enjoyed our new-found freedom, but as the euphoria began to fade did we see the maturing fruit of love in our lives and our churches? If we failed to grasp that love is not an optional extra but a command, we will not have noticed that the vacuum left when we rejected legalistic ways will in fact, if not filled with love, rob us again of our freedom and our joy.

Grace and love walk hand in hand – without love there would be no grace and without grace we cannot know God's love. In the same way that grace and love are partners, so love and obedience are inseparable.[2] God expressed his love through his grace; we must show our love by our obedience. Without obedience we cannot enjoy intimacy with God. We may proclaim that we are not under law, but can we truly claim to be under grace unless we are living under the rule of love? God's commitment of love for us is a constant, but to truly appreciate the relationship this love offers we must walk in the obedience that comes from our love for him.

It is only through love that the New Testament's teaching on grace makes sense. When Paul sets a standard for obedience to God that he compares to slavery, it is only meaningful if the motivation to obey is love.[3] An intellectualized love will never provide sufficient incentive for genuine lifestyle changes. The reason why Paul no longer wanted to do the things he sometimes couldn't help doing was the love he felt for God. He was prepared to struggle with himself in order to know intimacy with God – he longed to obey because he loved. With a heart obedient to the call to love – walking in love – he found the grace of God was available when he did do those things he couldn't help doing.[4] John echoes this when he talks of walking in the light. If we walk in the light of God's love, our desire for fellowship with God and his people will be greater than our desire for things that separate us from God and his people, and as long as we are walking in love, grace is available when we fail.[5]

Without love, the standard of commitment Christ requires of his followers looks radical, even dangerous. Jesus' take on holiness is 'If your hand causes you to sin, cut it off, or if your eye causes you to sin, gouge it out.'[6] Unless such teaching is interpreted in the context of love, it smacks of extreme fundamentalism, of sacrifice and punishment rather than grace. What Jesus is illustrating is the depth of love that he requires of us, not the actions through which we can earn his love. What wouldn't we do, what lengths wouldn't we go to, for those we truly love? If our offering is not love, in our attempt to live holy lives we will make unnecessary sacrifices when we should be enjoying God's grace – and disappointment and frustration will dominate our Christian experience.

It is when Christ's teaching is applied without love that we find the many evils, small and large, that are done in our churches and in the world in God's name. In love there is no room for the manipulation of consciences, the suppression of women or discrimination of any form. Nor is there a place for the rejection of fellow Christians because of their contentious doctrines, or for the persecution of those who don't share our beliefs. Without genuine love in our hearts these things take root in our lives and our congregations, and sadly they have sometimes characterized the church.

If our response to God's love and grace is not our own love, we may try to abolish rules and regulations but the result will not be freedom. We simply remove the framework by which we live and either drift away into lawlessness or eventually create a new set of rules. Without the benchmark of love, our church culture and our guidelines for Christian living can't fail to be influenced by the powerful negative shifts that have taken place in the way society thinks. We unwittingly reinvent the way we practise our religion to accommodate a contemporary culture that seems increasingly individualistic, selfish and greedy, where accountability has been replaced by blame, and community with competitiveness. In so doing, the church that should offer a counter-culture of love simply becomes an extension of the world – and the marginalized, the broken and the needy in our communities and our churches, those who should experience God's acceptance and love through his people, become even more alienated.

Without love, we may teach grace, but we eventually resort to an updated version of the hierarchy of sins for which, as young Christians, we mocked the older people in our churches. At best we simply reclassify things to make our definitions of sin more politically correct: divorce is probably OK after all; sex is still scary but we can now turn a blind eye to cohabitation before we marry; we still can't make up our mind about homosexuality. We strain out the gnat of individual actions and swallow the camel of lovelessness, and in so doing perpetuate the pain and power of sin and make a fool of the church in the eyes of the world.[7] We are able to recognize the splinter of 'worldliness' in the eyes of a brother or sister, but the all-pervading plank of lovelessness in our own eye is a 'worldliness' we are blind to. It is the fruits of this neo-legalism in our relationships that leave so many reeling with hurt and rejection at the fringes of the church.

Without love to fence us in, grace becomes a confused liberalism that blurs the differences between the world and the church. We are left like sheep scattered on the hillside, with the shepherds just as lost as their flocks.

We may have rediscovered the New Covenant but it is as dead as the old one unless we live out its central commands – to love God and to love each other. We may have a nice touchy-feely Christianity, but our emptying churches are half-full of people who are just as unhappy, disillusioned, stressed and lonely, or just as rich, successful and cheerful as the rest of the population. Love is the visible and tangible difference the church should make, but if church doesn't make a difference, what is the point?

A system of rules and regulations, no matter how liberal, can at best produce self-righteousness – at worst it fills us with a mixture of guilt and fear that leaves some in bondage and misery and leads others to walk out altogether. Many of us simply end up closing our minds to the confusing contradictions between the teaching on grace and the expectations put on us by our church culture about how we should actually live. Without love in the equation, the Christian life becomes an unattainable goal, so we give up thinking about it and consequently we miss out on the very thing that would make our religion alive and meaningful.

When my daughter was born, we became friends with a lady who shared the same ward as my wife and who had also just given birth to a baby girl. We kept in touch and one day she shared with us how terrible she had found the first few months alone at home with her child. Her pregnancy had been unpleasant and her labour long and painful, but none of this could really explain the feeling inside her that this baby was an unwanted intrusion into her life. When it woke her at night she tried to pretend it wasn't there; when it needed feeding she felt as if it was violating her body – and she struggled day and night with a feeling of guilt because she couldn't love her child. She wanted to, but every time she felt a spark of affection the child would make demands that she involuntarily resented. Slowly, though, things began to change. She was a very disciplined mother who fought against her negative emotions and spent extra time holding the child, talking to it, playing with it and fulfilling the duties she felt she had as a mother. Eventually, something deep inside her began to awaken, and a natural motherly instinct – an emotion much stronger than anything she had felt before – took over and filled her with love for her child. It was too contrary to her inclination to reject the child for her to have worked it up herself, and it was too powerful and alive to be a product of her imagination. It was a God-given response, as old as time itself, which made her know that she was indeed the child's mother.

The requirement to love God is a command we cannot avoid, but neither should we try to make ourselves love him. Any attempts to work up such feelings will produce, at best, the candy-floss love we have for our favourite celebrities and football teams – synthetic and short-lived – and at worst it will end in frustration and despair. We are not expected to conjure up feelings and emotions from nowhere. We are told that our love will be a natural, God-given response to the love he shows us, and he has given us the Spirit of the God of love to make his love real in our hearts.[8] It is the Holy Spirit within us who teaches us to love. He seals our adoption into God's family and calls to the innate need for God we all have and turns that need into love – a supernatural love that allows us to cry 'Abba, Father' in response to the Spirit's call.[9] Through the presence of the Holy Spirit we can begin to grasp the depth and breadth of God's love, and this will be reflected through the love in our lives and our churches.

When we read through the New Testament, we find that the dramatic manifestations of the Holy Spirit that we see at the beginning of Acts get less and less of a mention as we progress through the later books. Even as Ananias prays for Paul to receive the Holy Spirit, we see scales falling from his eyes but no tongues of fire or shaking buildings.[10] What we also find, though, is an amazing body of teaching prepared by Paul and other apostles: teaching that was revealed to them by the Spirit of God and with God's love stamped on every page. It isn't the events of Pentecost that have guided the church through the centuries but the work of the Counsellor who has revealed the love of God to his people. Could it be that as we moved beyond our own Pentecost we have lost sight of the love that was at the heart of the Spirit's outpouring? Have we looked instead for further blessing in the form of rousing worship, spiritual gifts and manifestations of God's power but ignored the voice of the Spirit who longs to make the love of God real in our lives?

Like the church at Ephesus, the churches of the northern hemisphere are full of dedicated, hard-working people who persevere even though they have been marginalized by society.[11] But if, like the church at Ephesus, we have lost our first love, we too are in danger of losing everything. If, as individuals, we are to leave the fringes of the church and if the church is to fulfil its God-given, love-driven role in society, we must repent of our lovelessness and mediocrity and find again the love, the desire for holiness and the passion and compassion we had at first. We must seek a love that is not based on religious idealism or couched in terms of clever doctrine, but which forms through the presence of God's Holy Spirit in our lives.

> *The only thing that counts is faith expressing itself through love.*
>
> Galatians 5:6b

Beyond the fringe

My wife is German, and when we first met I didn't speak a word of her language. Fortunately she spoke English so we were able to communicate. As I learned German, though, I realized that I had not been getting the whole picture: that language is much more than words. I found that there were things about my wife – her personality, her perspective on certain things, her culture – things that I could only understand properly in her own language. It took time and commitment to learn the language and there were frequent misunderstandings – but as I grew in knowledge of my wife I also grew in love.

The language that God uses to communicate with us is love, and it is with words of love that he writes his law on our hearts. A theoretical understanding of love will not allow us to know God, but when we seek him with all of our hearts, when we set aside time to meditate on his word, and as we take practical steps in obedience to love, the Holy Spirit will teach us a new vocabulary, the language of a deeper love that floods our hearts and makes a truly personal relationship with him possible.

Christ told us we can know the fullness of his loving nature; he intended us to lead fulfilled, rewarding lives and he promised us blessing, peace and joy through his love in even the most difficult circumstances. But he also underpinned these promises with the command to love – and the expectation that a love-motivated holiness would impact the way we live. If we have ignored this command, if we have conformed to the behavioural expectations of our church culture but neglected love and a love-driven desire for holiness, it would be premature to give up on God or settle for a dry and academic religion.

From our human perspective, the issue of holiness is challenging and confusing – a bewildering burden of archaic rules from the Bible and regulations from our churches. From God's perspective, though, holiness is the natural consequence of a heart that puts an uncompromising desire to know him above everything else. It is the faithfulness that comes from a heart that desires to be close to God. If we are to find our way through the maze of liberalism and legalism and allow the Holy Spirit to write the law of love in our lives, we need to come to God with a heart that is genuinely seeking, a heart that is honest about its doubts and weaknesses but willing to take the consequences of the demands that love makes on our lives.

Our church culture puts us under pressure to talk of loving relationships with God and each other when often we know in our hearts that there is little substance behind such talk. We need to be absolutely honest with ourselves and with God about our love. In practice many of us find the idea of loving God somewhat abstract and we fear to fall into the trap of forming an imaginary love. We fight a battle between feelings of inferiority and feelings of anger at those who make a big noise about love but who display no fruit of love in their behaviour towards us – and many of us carry scars from the times when we have been honest with others about our doubts. If God is love, however, this position of honest uncertainty has to be the best starting point for discovering a genuine experience of his love. We need to put aside our cynicism and hurts and come to Christ as the father with the demon-possessed child in the Gospel of Mark did: 'I do believe; help me overcome my unbelief.'[12]

We may feel let down by God and his people and find a contrast between the words of Christ and the daily reality in our lives and in our churches, but this does not mean God's promises are unreal or a relationship with God is unattainable. Instead, this contrast should spur us on in our search for something deeper. We will get it wrong many times, but God is looking for a desire to walk in love, for faltering steps along the path of love, rather than for perfection.

To the point

- Could a deeper love for God provide the key to the depth you are seeking in your spirituality?
- Do you really love God or have you confused love for him with love for your church?
- Have you discovered the freedom from feelings of guilt and the fear of people's opinions that is available to those who follow the way of love?
- Has your understanding of grace brought you closer to God?
- Would your experience of love have been deeper if you had placed less focus on the visible manifestations of the Spirit and on temporal blessings?
- How would a deeper love for God help you to cope with your disappointment with other Christians?

Meditation

The parable of the ten virgins

> *"At that time the kingdom of heaven will be like ten virgins who took their lamps and went out to meet the bridegroom. Five of them were foolish and five were wise. The foolish ones took their lamps but did not take any oil with them. The wise,*

however, took oil in jars along with their lamps. The bride-groom was a long time in coming, and they all became drowsy and fell asleep.

"At midnight the cry rang out: 'Here's the bridegroom! Come out to meet him!' Then all the virgins woke up and trimmed their lamps. The foolish ones said to the wise, 'Give us some of your oil; our lamps are going out.' 'No,' they replied, 'there may not be enough for both us and you. Instead, go to those who sell oil and buy some for yourselves.' But while they were on their way to buy the oil, the bridegroom arrived. The virgins who were ready went in with him to the wedding banquet. And the door was shut.

"Later the others also came. 'Sir! Sir!' they said. 'Open the door for us!' But he replied, 'I tell you the truth, I don't know you.'

"Therefore keep watch, because you do not know the day or the hour."

Matthew 25:1-13

The parable is clearly about being prepared for Christ's return, but it also tells us something about the relationships between the bridegroom and the wedding guests – between God and his people.

- The ten virgins, or bridesmaids as we might describe them today, presumably went out to greet the groom because they believed they knew him. In spite of this they were not guaranteed entry to the wedding party.
- All ten virgins slept – being attentive, well disciplined and active Christians is not the characteristic that will gain us recognition by the bridegroom. It was not what they did or didn't do that got five of them shut out of the party – it was what they didn't have.
- Today we might use the image of teenage music fans waiting for the arrival of their pop idol. Those whose

'love is real' arrive three days earlier and take sleeping bags and enough to eat and drink; others turn up on the off-chance.

- If I am invited to a party and don't respond appropriately, it probably reflects my feelings for the host more than anything. If I love the host, nothing will prevent me from attending the party. The thought of the second coming of Christ, or even of our own death, often fills us with fear and dread. It is only by loving God that we can prepare for either, and it is only the certainty found in God's love that can really conquer fear.

- We start our Christian lives on fire with love and enthusiasm, but as time goes on our flame begins to dwindle: if we are not careful our oil dries up. We are still waiting for the bridegroom, we are still part of the wedding party – but is our flame still burning? It is only through a growing relationship with God that the oil of our love will remain alight.

- The echoes of the door slamming shut and the call of the bridegroom, 'I never knew you,' sound hard and fill us with fearful thoughts. Jesus was very clear that though we may do many things in his name, from prophecy to miracles, if we have ignored the will of the Father we will not be known.[13] The will of the Father is that we love.

> *Yet I hold this against you: You have forsaken your first love. Remember the height from which you have fallen! Repent and do the things you did at first. If you do not repent, I will come to you and remove your lampstand from its place.*
>
> Revelation 2:4-5

> *Someone told him, "Your mother and brothers are standing outside wanting to speak to you." He replied to him, "Who is*

*my mother, and who are my brothers?" Pointing to his disci-
ples, he said, "Here are my mother and my brothers. For
whoever does the will of my Father in heaven is my brother
and sister and mother."*

Matthew 12:47-50

*"Not everyone who says to me, 'Lord, Lord,' will enter the
kingdom of heaven, but only he who does the will of my Father
who is in heaven. Many will say to me on that day, 'Lord,
Lord, did we not prophesy in your name, and in your name
drive out demons and perform many miracles?' Then I will tell
them plainly, 'I never knew you. Away from me, you evildo-
ers!'*

Matthew 7:21-23

Prayer

Father God, while I have been busy with my life the
flame of love for you in my heart has cooled and grown
faint. Forgive me for my lukewarm heart. I give it to you,
Lord, and ask that through your Holy Spirit you will
rekindle my love for you and for your church. Melt the
hardness that has formed where love should be, show
me the idols in my life and make knowing you my
heart's desire. Let those in my church and those around
me see your love and grace in my life. Amen.

Notes

[1] 2 Kgs. 22:1 – 23:30.
[2] Jn. 14:15.
[3] Rom. 6:1-23.
[4] Rom. 7:15-25.

5 1 Jn. 1:5 – 2:2.
6 Mt. 5:27-30.
7 Mt. 23:24.
8 1 Jn. 4:19.
9 Rom. 8:14-16.
10 Acts 9:17-19.
11 Rev. 2:1-7.
12 Mk. 9:24.
13 Mt. 7:21-23.

As I have loved you

For anyone who does not love his brother, whom he has seen, cannot love God, whom he has not seen. And he has given us this command: Whoever loves God must also love his brother.
1 John 4:20b-21

Helen was a member of a church youth club that I used to run with a couple of friends. At the time she was 12 years old and came from a very difficult background. Her father had physically abused her when she was small. He was now homeless and lived rough around the town. He had regular run-ins with the police for crimes ranging from drunk and disorderly to indecent exposure, and because all the locals knew him, Helen went through hell at school with her classmates. She had been coming to the club for a while and was in many ways one of our favourites – a special kid with loads of character, a great sense of humour and a loving heart.

On one unforgettable Sunday evening I arrived at church to find the doors locked and Helen sitting on the front step in tears. When she was eventually able to compose herself enough to speak, she pointed to a note on the door that explained that due to unforseen circumstances the youth club had been closed indefinitely. It didn't take me long to find out that a leadership disagreement in the church that weekend had split the congregation in two – consequently the church's extensive programme of community activity had been shut down with immediate effect. I was angry about the closure but what really made my blood boil was that kids like Helen, who had believed the church to be a safe haven of love and acceptance, were so callously dmped.

The young people weren't the only casualties. The church had at one time been quite outstanding in its love, and the devastation that the split caused amongst the members was as great as their love had once been. Sadly there are many who can recount similar stories and who, like me, ask why it is that the body of Christ on earth, the living representation of God's love for humankind, so often becomes a place of hurt, anger and bitterness.

If we take a careful look at the fringes of our church communities we will see that a very high proportion of people have arrived there not because of their rebellion or sin, but as a result of the hurt and rejection they have experienced at the hands of their fellow Christians. Some hide in the anonymity of the church margins because their commitment and hard work have not been recognized – and consequently frustration, resentment and eventually pain have replaced their motivation. Some are there because they have been attacked by a jealous brother or sister; others are there because they have 'failed' or 'sinned' in the eyes of their church and they have retreated from the stinging bite of judgmental and critical attitudes.

It sometimes seems as if almost everybody who starts on their Christian journey full of enthusiasm is destined at some point to end up nursing the wounds they have received at the hands of the church community. Hurt and disappointed because of the lovelessness they have encountered, many withdraw into a purpose-built shell of pain. Some try to remain involved but struggle with anger, bitterness and a battered self-confidence; others leave and attempt to practise their faith in the safety of their own homes.

Those who would try to explain away falling church membership as a refining or pruning process would see how incredibly short-sighted this view is if they examined the hurting population at the margins of our churches, or if they talked to those who have given up and left altogether. If this is the goats being sorted from the sheep, an awful lot of sheep are being placed in the wrong pen.[1]

Why is it that the children of the God of love have so much difficulty loving each other? Jesus is very clear about the standard of love he sets for us: we must love each other as he loved us.[2] This is the new commandment that was meant to be at the heart of church life: the only thing that would make it possible for such a diverse group of people with all their strengths and weaknesses, failings and eccentricities to come together as living stones in a spiritual house – into the church. No longer are we to love merely as we love ourselves; we are to have the sacrificial love of Jesus for our fellow believers.

He meant this, above all else, to be the characteristic that made his church stand out in the world. It was part of his plan that through the love that Christians have for each other the world would see him. It was on the basis of this love that our message would have credibility: the platform on which we were to preach the gospel to the ends of the earth; a love to die for and a love to live for; a love that banishes fear and makes us fruitful and joyful regardless of our circumstances. There is no greater love than that of someone who lays down his life for his friends – we quote this verse for our heroes, but this is the standard of love that God requires us to have for each other. And it is only as we obey this command that Jesus can call us his friends.[3]

One of the biggest shocks for me as a young Christian was leaving home and finding that people outside the church could be just as loving and caring as those on the inside. In my naivety I was astounded to discover that there was a sense of community outside the church, and close bonds of friendship that frequently exceeded what I had experienced from my fellow Christians. I found a tolerance and understanding, even with my beliefs, that I had rarely encountered amongst the Christians I knew at that time. It wasn't the bright lights and the high-life that tempted me – it was the need to belong and the open arms with which I was accepted, as I was, by my new-found friends.

How many young people turn their backs on church when they leave home and find amongst their friends and colleagues greater acceptance, greater honesty and loyalty and fewer behavioural expectations? I was warned by Christians who rarely ventured out of their cloistered evangelical existence that friendship with non-Christians can neither be as genuine nor as deep as friendships in the church. But this simply isn't true. In a world where the consequences of greed and selfishness seem to be ever more apparent, the need for belonging is promoting a sense of kindred spirit amongst many, especially young people. Common fears, shared concerns about freedom and justice, and growing awareness of the pain and suffering in a world we are destroying lead to close bonds of friendship across backgrounds and beliefs, bonds that many within the church would envy.

Non-believing friends can let you down and they can hurt you, but no more than many of those at the outer reaches of our churches have experienced at the hands of their Christian brothers and sisters.

We talk so much about our love for each other. We preach about it and claim to have something very special, but if this is true, why are there so many damaged and hurt people at the fringe who were once at the heart of church life? I have asked this question many times in my frustration, and one reply I have often heard is that 'as Christians we make ourselves more vulnerable and we are therefore bound to hurt each other'. Although this contains an element of truth, it is in fact an admission of failure that implies that those who make themselves vulnerable do so in a hostile rather than a loving environment, where clearly vulnerability and therefore genuine love are not the norm. We come up with excuses such as 'We're just forgiven sinners' or 'You have to be realistic, you can't live in each other's pockets.' We talk about practicalities and common sense and don't realize that because we are disobeying Jesus' command to love, we are robbing ourselves of the love and quality of relationships that would give meaning and value to our experience of church.

We have confused love for our churches with love for each other and have lost the very thing that made the church recognizable as the bride and body of Christ. We say we love, and to some degree we do, but both the casualties at the fringes of our churches and our loss of credibility in the world bear witness to the truth – that like our love for the Father, our love for each other is lukewarm. Few of us would deny that the sort of unconditional love Jesus talks of is what we long for deep down inside. It was Christ's teaching on love that first attracted many of us to the church in the first place.

And though we found something of that love during our early days as Christians, the vision of love we once shared has turned sour and ended in hurt. Why? Because as a church we have accepted second-best and redefined the standard of our love to accommodate our human fears and desires. Like our love for God, our love for each other is something we take for granted: we assume we love without ever really looking at the standard of love laid down by Christ. We bury our heads in the sand of church activity and lose sight of his call and command to love.

When we look at our churches, time and time again we see passionate and dedicated people giving of themselves and reaching out to each other in love. But as soon as a project begins to bear fruit, jealousy and other loveless behaviour takes over and crushes the work and the heart of the people behind it. As hurting people we begin to put up walls, sometimes anger and bitterness take root – and gone is the vulnerability that is essential for loving relationships to develop. It is a bitter cycle of destruction that leads to pain, fear and damaged self-esteem – hurt people hurting each other and a poison in the body of Christ that cripples not just the individuals concerned but the whole church.

It was my hurt, anger and frustration with the church that guided my pen when I first started to write. At some point, though, it dawned on me that while love and vulnerability have always been pet themes of mine, my hardness and anger were in fact also part of this cycle of destruction. I realized that they had made me just as unloving and just as guilty as I accused the church of being – and those who had behaved in a hard and unloving way towards me had usually done so because of their own painful and negative experiences. The first victim of lovelessness is love itself, which escapes through the wound of our hurts and makes us just as much a part of the vicious circle of lovelessness, rejection, fear and hurt as those we accuse.

When I look back over the occasions when I have been hurt, or when I talk to others who have been through their own painful experiences, there are common themes that emerge: powerlessness, feelings of injustice, not being valued as we should be, having our love trampled under foot. The normal response is to cut ourselves off from fellowship and lick our wounds alone – even if we continue to be present at church services, we withdraw in spirit. We make excuses for people's behaviour and try to write it off as normal, but eventually most of us put up our barriers and our 'Keep away' signs. Our hurt and our anger blind us to the goodness in God and his people: they make us impervious to love, stifle our faith and 'grieve the Holy Spirit'.[4]

As I wrote of these things, I realized that the emotions I was describing were the same as those that Christ must have experienced from his birth in a stable through to his death on a cross. In making himself vulnerable through love, he had laid aside his power, he had suffered terrible injustice, he was rejected, his love was trampled underfoot and his true value not recognized. When, as a young person, I declared from the bottom of my heart that I would follow Jesus, it was to these things that I said I would follow him. There is no way round it. No matter how righteous our anger is, regardless of how deep our hurt is or how justified our indignation, the call to follow is, above all else, a call to love. And if we are to love like Jesus there will be no escaping some of the pain he experienced. We may feel we have suffered a great injustice, but there was no greater injustice than Christ's crucifixion. Perhaps this is part of what Paul means when he talks of us being united with Christ in his death.[5]

The call to lay down our life in love is also a call to lay down our pride, our ambitions, the status we have in the church, perhaps even our doctrinal position, in the name of love. When we are hurt or treated badly by fellow believers, the first thing we reach out for is our rights, because we feel as if our 'God-given rights' have been violated. But did we not surrender our rights when we came to God? We have been humiliated, we have lost our dignity, we have had our love thrown back in our face. But what right have we to complain; what right have we to a comfortable and pain-free existence; what right do we have to better treatment than Jesus? 'But look how badly I have been treated, look what they have done to me,' we cry – and 'Look how badly they treated me' is the loving and gentle reply from the cross.

It is tragic that most of the persecution that Christians in the West experience comes from within their own churches. But as long as the commands and example of Christ are still a stumbling-block, as long as those who don't fall down at the call to love are tripped up on their own anger and bitterness, this will not change. If we are to love as he loved us, if we are to break the cycle of hurt in our lives that is behind much of our disappointment, we must learn to remain vulnerable and to love and forgive in the face of scorn and rejection at the hands of those who claim to be our own people.

I have often wondered what temptation Jesus struggled with most as a man. As I have become older and experienced some of life's injustices, I have come to suspect that it might have been the temptation to lash out at those who rejected his love, and to punish those who hurt the weak and the vulnerable people closest to him. The thing that made Jesus' reaction different to mine was his intimate relationship with the God who is by nature love. He knew of a deeper unconditional love:

love for love's sake that could look rejection in the eye and not stop loving. So confident was he of the power of this love that he allowed it to lead him to the cross, where he laid down his life in the ultimate act of vulnerability.

Everything we have and everything we are promised as Christians stems from God's love – our forgiveness, our healing, our joy, our peace, and the gift of his Holy Spirit. But until we start to love and forgive our brother as we are commanded to we will only enjoy a shadow of these things. Unless we are willing to look for something deeper than the veneer of love we have, we will be unable to appreciate the extent of God's love for us. Unless there is a revolution in brotherly love the church will never see the revival it is hoping and praying for. If we open our hearts and are willing to take a step along the road of love we will find, like Christ, that instead of lashing out we can also forgive. We will find the healing of our hurts and our lives will minister the love and forgiveness of Christ and bring healing and awakening to others, and our churches.

A short time ago a lady in our church offered to babysit so that my wife and I could have a rare evening out together. I didn't know her well but she had always struck me as somebody with a gentle spirit. It was only when we were talking after our evening out that I recognized in her the signs of somebody who had been hurt by her experiences in the church. This wasn't the subject of our discussion, but she obviously recognized the same scars in me – and a few days later she gave me a long, handwritten letter in which she told of the pain and the rejection she had suffered, of how God had spoken to her and how she was slowly finding healing.

She was clearly still very fragile, and although she didn't really know me at all (that evening was our first real conversation) she had responded to the call to love and had made herself vulnerable to me. It is hard to explain the impact of her letter. It was as if a gentle hand had very carefully pulled aside the thorns, taking the risk of being hurt herself, and allowed me to see that there was still something of value in me, something that wanted to love and forgive. I began to see how the briers that had wrapped themselves around my heart had damaged my self-esteem, how anger was hurting me more than anybody else, and very slowly I saw that I did have the strength to let go of these feelings and make myself vulnerable again. She didn't write any complicated spiritual formula or even give any advice, she just made herself vulnerable – and the healing power of love was able to begin its work.

Jesus was also rejected and hurt by his own people; he too lived at the fringes of his community. But when he called us to follow him he also taught us about love – the most powerful tool for healing that exists. When those who understand the destructive power of lovelessness begin to reach out to each other in love, we will find that it is those at the fringe who are bringing blessing to the church. As we learn to love in spite of our hurts, as we discover love for love's sake – love for God's sake – we will find that we are channels of God's healing for the church and the world outside. When we learn to draw from the well of God's love we will find a force that can dissolve our frustration and disappointment, heal our hurts, bring back our children and change the church from a smouldering ember to a blazing light.

The entire law is summed up in a single command: "Love your neighbour as yourself." If you keep on biting and devouring each other, watch out or you will be destroyed by each other.
Galatians 5:14-15

Beyond the fringe

During the war in the Balkans in the 90s, we invited a family of Bosnian Muslims to live with us. They had suffered terribly during the siege of Sarajevo and they arrived with physical signs of malnutrition and the emotional trauma that comes from having witnessed some of the darkest evil that human nature can produce. To add to their pain, their father remained trapped in Sarajevo, exposed to the merciless bombardment of Serbian artillery. It is difficult to describe the horrific damage that war does to people, but it is rarely limited to the symptoms of starvation and gunshot wounds. It can light the fuse on a Catherine wheel of hatred that spirals into ever greater intensity: hatred that is blind to common sense, that eventually turns the victim into an aggressor; into the very thing they most hate.

I arrived home from work one day to find one of our Bosnian guests, a teenage boy, leaning out of the window with an air rifle in his hands. We lived on a small farm and used the weapon to deal with rats and other vermin. However, as I walked through the door he pulled the trigger and the screams of pain from outside made it apparent that it was his sister he had shot and not a farmyard pest. I have rarely felt so overwhelmed by hopelessness as I witnessed this scene, as we comforted this young girl whose pain went much deeper than the severe haematoma on her leg. Just a few evenings before, the boy had told me the heart-rending story of how she had been shot through the shoulder by a gunman in the infamous Sniper Alley. He spoke of his own pain at seeing her hurt and how he, his father and some friends had gone out seeking revenge: how they had found a couple of Serbian civilians and beaten them nearly to death with clubs and rifle butts. I could understand this reaction, but it was when I saw him pointing a gun at the sister he was so passionate about protecting and avenging that I realized the true depth of damage that hatred and hurt had caused in his life.

When Christ broke the cycle of death, he also released the power of his love to us so that we could break the cycle of hatred and destruction in our lives and in our world. Sadly, love is an area where we are most vulnerable to attack and failure, and unloving behaviour has a well-established bridgehead in our churches. Just as they do in the world, painful situations spiral out of control. We may not use the weapons of war, but it is sometimes unbelievable how seemingly small incidents can trigger a chain reaction that brings a whirlwind of destruction to our lives and leaves a trail of 'collateral damage' throughout the church community. Through rejection and hurt, love is replaced with the blunt instrument of hardness and anger, and a pattern of loveless behaviour is set in motion that robs us of our relationships with each other and our relationship with God.

This cycle can be broken, though, and a powerful cascade of love and healing, of restoration and wholeness, can take its place. If, through forgiveness and love, we disarm the hurt, anger and bitterness in our lives, those of us who have retreated to the margins of our churches because of our hurts are the people best positioned to initiate the process. It seems unnatural, it goes against the grain to forgive, but there is no alternative – we need to meet the hurtful and unjust behaviour we have encountered with unconditional forgiveness. It looks like an impossible step over a great chasm of fear, but as we step out we will be surprised how God will open the floodgates of his love in our lives – a supernatural love that changes our very nature, taking away the desire to retaliate and lash out and replacing it with forgiveness and with a love that heals our pain and dissolves our anger. It might not happen overnight, but from the moment we set our hearts to forgive, things will begin to change, and one day we will suddenly notice that the weight of negative feelings that has burdened our spirit is gone.

The lovelessness that is central to many of our disappointments with the church is also the missing piece in the puzzle of our failed witness. In a world where a loveless church has been party to many terrible acts – where in the minds of many the church is linked to things like colonialism, apartheid, the crusades and the oppression and exploitation of the developing world by the Christian west – the only way to regain the right to be heard is through the genuine love of God in our hearts and in our churches. When the sacrificial love of Christ is reflected in his people, the light of the God of love will shine powerfully in the darkness of our broken society. Love is our credibility in a world where family life is crumbling and relationships, like people, are disposable: it is the only platform from which we will be taken seriously.

At the moment we may be acutely aware of the pain we have experienced at the hands of other Christians, but if we risk forgiving we will find that our negative experiences become a training ground where we can grow in love. Through the intense relationships of our small Christian communities we have the opportunity to learn to cope with the feelings of powerlessness, injustice and rejection that Christ felt. When we begin to love and forgive in the face of these things, we can start to taste the freedom and joy of true relationships with God and our fellow Christians. When those with broken spirits begin to join hands, to encourage and build each other in love, Christ's love will spill over into the church and the world around us and offer a way out of the cycle of hatred that is destroying so many.

To the point

- Do you recognize people in your church who feel disappointed or marginalized?
- Could it lead you to feel more included and loved yourself if you allowed these people to see your love and your need for love?
- Are you aware of people you may have hurt because of anger or pain in your life?
- Could you help make the church feel more like a 'spiritual home' for yourselves and others if you risked opening yourself in love?
- Can you truly say that your love for fellow Christians exceeds the love you experience in secular society?
- Do you make members in your church feel as if they belong?
- Have you experienced the joy of relationships unhampered by anger and hurt?
- Have you tasted the healing and sense of release you find when you start to forgive?
- Have you discovered the patience, understanding and tolerance for other people that comes as you recognize your own need of grace?

Meditation

The parable of the unmerciful servant

> *"Therefore, the kingdom of heaven is like a king who wanted to settle accounts with his servants. As he began the settlement, a*

man who owed him ten thousand talents was brought to him. Since he was not able to pay, the master ordered that he and his wife and his children and all that he had be sold to repay the debt.

"The servant fell on his knees before him. 'Be patient with me,' he begged, 'and I will pay back everything.' The servant's master took pity on him, cancelled the debt and let him go.

"But when that servant went out, he found one of his fellow-servants who owed him a hundred denarii. He grabbed him and began to choke him. 'Pay back what you owe me!' he demanded.

"His fellow-servant fell to his knees and begged him, 'Be patient with me, and I will pay you back.'

"But he refused. Instead, he went off and had the man thrown into prison until he could pay the debt. When the other servants saw what had happened, they were greatly distressed and went and told their master everything that had happened.

"Then the master called the servant in. 'You wicked servant,' he said, 'I cancelled all that debt of yours because you begged me to. Shouldn't you have had mercy on your fellow-servant just as I had on you?' In anger his master turned him over to the jailers to be tortured, until he should pay back all he owed.

"This is how my heavenly Father will treat each of you unless you forgive your brother from your heart."

Matthew 18:23-35

- Forgiveness and mercy are love's children; we may be able to forgive without loving but we cannot truly love if we are not forgiving and merciful. As our love reflects our Christlikeness, so does our readiness to forgive, and in the same way that lovelessness is a destructive form of worldliness in the church, its twin – our lack of forgiveness – is equally damaging.
- Our sense of justice and fair play demands that we be vindicated when we are accused. We look for

punishment and revenge: our adversary should apologize and experience the same humiliation as we have. But not forgiving is not an option if we claim to follow Christ. The only string attached to payment of the servant's debt was that he too should forgive those who owed him. God expects the same of us – if we don't forgive our brother or sister we will not be forgiven.

- The call to love our enemies is also a call to forgive them. This is not a theoretical love but the heart-wrenching love that took Jesus to the cross for us when we were his enemies.

- There is a virtuous circle of supernatural love available to us when we begin to forgive and love. When we put aside the lovelessness that grieves the Spirit of God we will find that the low-hanging spiritual fruit of God's love within us will make forgiving and loving part of our nature.

- The master did not deny the existence of the debt – he cancelled it. Love does not deny the crime – it looks it in the face and still forgives.

- Our worship, our fellowship and our communion with God cannot be real unless we have fellowship with our brothers and sisters. Paul goes so far as to attribute the weakness and sickness in the church at Corinth to the loveless way they took communion. Could it also affect the health of our churches?

- If we are to follow the example of Jesus in love and vulnerability, we will only survive if we also follow his example of forgiveness and mercy. Forgiving a person does not take away the hurt, but it does allow love in so that the healing process can begin.

- Forgiveness is a great equalizer – when we all genuinely acknowledge our own need for forgiveness we find the freedom of having nothing more to prove and no reputation to live up to.

- When we look back at the discarded skins of our
  unforgiving nature we can see just how bound we
  were by our negativity and our critical behaviour. No
  matter how justifiable, it was an emotional straitjacket that just dragged us down.
- The hardest person to forgive is often ourselves. We
  are easily deceived out of God's grace by a perverse
  twist in our nature that tells us we can make everything better by feeling bad and punishing ourselves.
  To appreciate God's forgiveness we must forgive ourselves too.

*"A new commandment I give you: Love one another. As I have
loved you, so you must love one another. By this all men will
know that you are my disciples, if you love one another."*

John 13:34-35

*Let no debt remain outstanding, except the continuing debt to
love one another, for he who loves his fellow-man has fulfilled
the law.*

Romans 13:8

*"For if you forgive men when they sin against you, your heav-
enly Father will also forgive you. But if you do not forgive men
their sins, your Father will not forgive your sins."*

Matthew 6:14-15

*And do not grieve the Holy Spirit of God, with whom you were
sealed for the day of redemption. Get rid of all bitterness, rage
and anger, brawling and slander, along with every form of
malice. Be kind and compassionate to one another, forgiving
each other, just as in Christ God forgave you.*

Ephesians 4:30-32

Prayer

Father, help me to be willing to have my heart broken in love. Teach me to bring restoration to my relationships through the forgiveness that your love enables, and healing to others through the love that you release in me. Lead your church to ever greater depths of love and mercy. Amen.

Notes

[1] Mt. 25:31-46.
[2] Jn. 13:34-35.
[3] Jn. 15:12-14.
[4] Eph. 4:30-32.
[5] Rom. 6:5-14.

6

Serving the Lord or robbing God?

But Samuel replied: "Does the LORD delight in burnt offerings and sacrifices as much as in obeying the voice of the LORD? To obey is better than sacrifice, and to heed is better than the fat of rams."

1 Samuel 15:22

Like so many Christians who find themselves disappointed and on the fringes of church life, I tried for years to serve God in the church. I was involved in youth work, community projects, evangelism, a bit of preaching and even theological studies: the whole gamut of things that committed young Christians get involved in, plus a bit more. For much of my early life nearly all of my free time was taken up with church-related activity, and those who took my enthusiasm and energy as a sign of a promising future have probably felt let down. I don't think I was particularly ambitious, but with the benefit of hindsight I can see that I was certainly driven by a strong desire for acceptance, and my work was always conducted as if I had something to prove.

When I look back and examine that period of my life with honesty, very few of the activities I was involved in produced the harvest I had expected. In spite of my best efforts, many of the things I turned my hand to eventually just petered out, and some ended in strife and hurt for those involved – hardly any produced lasting fruit. For many of us this experience seems to be the norm rather than the exception. There are so many dedicated, hard-working Christians who slave away relentlessly at one project after another – sometimes even working to the detriment of their health or their families – but with little to show for their labour. Unless they are particularly resilient it will ultimately only be a matter of time before disillusionment, jealousy or lack of recognition on the part of fellow Christians, or some form of burn-out will drive them to the fringes of church life.

In many ways, though, it was these negative experiences during those years of 'faithful' but relatively unfruitful service that forced me to acknowledge that the cloak of Christian culture I had subscribed to did not cover my spiritual nakedness. My years of toil in the church, doing what I sincerely believed was expected of me as a Christian, had in practice led me further and further into a spiritual desert. It has taken me a long time to grasp that even though my dedication came from a heartfelt belief that this was how to please God, much of what I did was simply conforming to the culture and practices of church life. It was not, as I had believed, a walk along the narrow and difficult road that would lead me closer to Christ.

My commitment may even at times have been exemplary, but at the end of the day the works were usually my works and it was the praise and acceptance of fellow Christians that touched my heart rather than a deepening relationship with God. Though it was regarded as a sign of following Christ, much of it was in fact following an established pattern of Christian behaviour that served the church but not God. I am not saying that the projects I undertook were necessarily wrong in themselves, but the service that I had believed would take me closer to God had in reality at times been a barrier to seeking, knowing and obeying him.

New Christians generally find themselves very quickly drawn into the activity of their churches. Although this may help them initially to feel part of the church family, it can also lead to wrong beliefs and expectations. Subconsciously we come to equate our obedient service in the church with the expression of our relationship with God. We confuse seeking to *know* God with working *for* God, and believe our commitment to following Christ is lived out through our energetic involvement in church programmes. Our activity gets us into the flow of church life but we frequently become too busy to notice that what we are living isn't the intimate walk with God we expected.

Pleasing God is interpreted as serving him in the church, and spiritual growth is measured in terms of our activity: busy, active Christians are growing and fruitful Christians. Spiritual maturity is defined by the number of years we have spent in dedicated service, by the theological colleges we attended and the positions of responsibility we have held. In some churches there is even a sort of career path we can follow to 'maturity' where, if we are faithful in the small things – the cleaning rota, Sunday school, youth club – we might eventually be trusted in greater things: preaching, the diaconate and eldership.

This may give us enough satisfaction to keep us happy and committed, but when things go wrong we notice that it doesn't add up to the life of joy and peace that the Bible promises. We become caught in a very clever form of deception: we expect God to bless us because we are busy in his church, but we become too preoccupied to discover the blessing he would give us if our works were derived from our closeness to him. God's desire is that we know him. As long as working to please God takes the place of getting to know God, our sincere commitment to good works can even become a subtle form of unfaithfulness, and before we know it, the spark of love we felt when we first came to Christ has been extinguished.

Those of us who grew up in Christian homes or who have been believers for a long time are perhaps particularly susceptible to a work-driven church life. We feel intensely guilty if we are not at every meeting and part of every project team, and this guilt often takes the pleasure out of the very activity we feel we should be involved in. It certainly comes between us and God, because there can be no place for guilt in a relationship built on grace. At times we feel enslaved by our sense of duty, and an honest examination of the fruit in our lives reveals that though our desire may be to serve God, it is a conscience motivated by church culture that we are actually serving. Although the stress of our activity may cause us to sacrifice our health and our relationships, sadly it is usually only when things collapse or when we fail in some way that we notice we are not one step closer to knowing God. For many children of Christian parents this guilt becomes like a straitjacket that they throw off aggressively as soon as they leave home.

Perhaps one of the most powerful incentives for Christian activity is our desire to belong and our need for affirmation. In a loving environment this can be channelled into building strong relationships and can help us to grow in receiving and giving love, but where there is little love, our search for recognition becomes a treadmill of service that burns us out and destroys the very relationships we are looking for. Like the rest of society, the church is full of people hungry for love. But where church life is activity-driven, instead of finding love through our relationships with God and each other we try to earn it in the form of praise and approval for our works. When we are successful and we receive the recognition we seek, we are spurred on to greater projects; when our labour goes unnoticed, or even fails, we work twice as hard because the only thing affirmed is our need to prove ourselves.

The family of the church has an important role to play in establishing both our identity and our self-image. There is nothing as effective in creating a healthy self-esteem as a caring group of family or friends encouraging each other and actively building one another up in love as God planned it.[1] However, if we don't have the intimacy with God that allows us to draw on his love for ourselves and for each other, and if we don't take the time to form close relationships with fellow Christians, we will never find the sense of self-worth and belonging we need. When we exchange Christian duty for love we also exchange a true revelation of the value God sees in us for a theoretical knowledge that can never lead to a positive self-image. When we make our commitment to the church a substitute for our relationships, our Christian programmes will eventually become like the children that keep an ailing marriage together. When they leave home – when our good works are no longer needed – we notice that we got it wrong, by which time our relationship is in tatters.

If we seek acceptance through our service in the church, disappointment will be inevitable. If we build our self-esteem on the basis of successful church projects, we will eventually develop an acute sense of failure. It is the hurt, rejection and disillusionment that many of us experience when we don't find the love we were looking for, the crash when we finally burn out, or the hurt we inflict on each other when our ambitious projects fail, that cause many of us to give up and move away from involvement in mainstream church life. And because our relationship with God was built on a premise of service and activity, we find that instead of the expected growth the opposite has taken place – there is in fact very little left of the faith we once had. As long as our heads are full of the buzz of our activity we are fine, but if we find our activity is no longer needed, if somebody does it better, or if we fail, in the silence that remains we discover a spiritual vacuum in our lives.

Another danger is the self-righteousness that so easily develops when we fill our Christian lives with 'good works'. Nobody is immune to the risk of feeling too good about themselves when things go well, and when we do, we subconsciously lose sight of our need for grace. Why is it that we so often fall back to trying to justify ourselves by our works? We don't consciously reject God's grace but we are effectively denying its adequacy for us at the moment we begin to 'earn' our favour with God. It is only a loving heart that will please God, and the service that results directly from our love for him – not working ourselves silly trying to run a youth club or outreach programme for our churches. With our mouths we proclaim that he is God Almighty, but from our actions one could be forgiven for thinking that we believe he can't get by without us. Unless our service is the fruit of our love for God, it will inevitably come between us and God, and we will probably sacrifice other relationships in the process.

Similarly, as long as our service in the church is seen as the practical expression of our obedience to God, we risk disobeying him. If we equate obeying God with our dedication to work, we may fulfil the letter of the law of church culture, but we will neglect the spirit of the law of God that requires of us, first and foremost, a faithful and loving heart. If our sacrifice is our labour, like the children of Israel we will bring our regular offerings and tithes and we may even feel good about ourselves, but if this becomes a substitute for love we are effectively robbing God of the offering he requires. If we have been slaving away in our churches we may feel as if we have done our bit and paid our dues. But serving the church does not exempt us from the command to love each other, witnessing to the lost does not negate the command to love the world, and preaching the word of God can never replace the command to love God. We must find the courage to examine objectively and honestly the programmes we are committed to and establish whether or not they are truly from God. If we see fruitlessness but much hard work, if we find hurt and burnt-out casualties at the fringes of our churches, if we see a world outside the church that will not cross the threshold of our buildings, we must ask ourselves if it is really God we are serving.

If our works are to bear fruit they must stem from, rather than replace, our search to know, love and obey God. It was because King David was more concerned about obeying God than being king that God chose him as king. It was because of his obedience that he could be so close to God that he knew his heart, and it was because David's heart was in tune with God's that he was entrusted with leading God's people – because God knew he would love them and lead them as he would himself. David's knowledge of God's heart was the basis of his selection, his anointing, and the work he did as king. David's life revolved around his love for God and he sought God in all that he did.

David's strength as a leader was that he never confused serving the God of Israel with serving the people or the state of Israel. He could only achieve this because although he had a great love for his nation and culture, his love for God was always greater. He was far from inactive – his psalms alone are a lifetime's work for most people – but because God was his first love and obedience to God was his highest priority, his works bore fruit for generations to come. When, hundreds of years later, his descendant Jesus was tempted by the devil, he too made it clear that it was only God that he would serve, and his service has also brought fruit down to the present day.[2] It is sometimes easy to get the impression that God has his favourites – people like David – but it has nothing to do with favouritism. It is a heart that obeys out of love and loves out of obedience – a heart after God's heart – that is the very thing that God wishes for all of us.

We are often a little like children trying to please their parents. My kids love to make things for me, and over the years these presents have gradually become more and more sophisticated. When they were small children I was delighted at the pictures they brought home from school for me, the models they made and the little notes they left on my pillow. Like many parents, I have a box in the loft full of their little love-gifts. But now they are older they are slowly beginning to realize that it is not what they do for me that makes me love them; they know I love them and they are confident that I will never stop loving them. They are starting to understand that it's not what they can do for me but the friendship they have with me, the intimacy, the conversation and closeness that I value most.

If my children were to spend all their lives working like mad to please me, it would indicate that there was something very wrong either with my love for them or with their ability to understand and receive my love. Or it could be that they simply weren't standing still long enough to hear and see that I love them. Of course, it is nice when they wait on me, but I would be a terrible father if I measured their love for me on the basis of their service. Although service may originate from a sincere desire to please and to obey, it is no basis for a relationship. God loved the little pictures we brought him as children: but now we are older what he wants first and foremost is a relationship with us. If we are still bringing pictures, our love has failed to mature. He sent his Son to die so that we could enjoy communion with him, and he saved us so that love could be mutual, but if we have tried too hard to please him through our service our love will have been stifled by our effort.

How would we feel if God were to say to us, 'All I want of you is that you get on with life and spend all of your free time getting to know me and being kind and just to people around you. I don't want you working in the youth club or preaching on Sundays – but meditating, reading the Bible, spending time in prayer and walking humbly with me'?[3] Would we feel guilty because we were 'doing nothing' and even annoyed that we didn't get to be part of the action? If we have learned love through obedience we will recognize the honour of being allowed to 'do nothing'. If love is our motivation, what could be better than to be told to spend time with God? Jesus made it absolutely clear to Martha that Mary had chosen the better way, simply sitting at the feet of Jesus and enjoying his presence.[4] She wasn't better than Martha, she wasn't his favourite, but she had chosen the way that allowed them to enjoy mutual love.

I was struck a few months ago by a radio interview with Sister Frances Dominica, Deputy Mother Superior of a convent in Oxford and founder of the first children's hospice in the world, Helen House. The hospice has become a beacon that shines out the compassion and tenderness of Christ to the whole community, and sends a powerful message about his love to some of the most hurting people in the world. Indeed, everybody who has come across the work of Helen House cannot fail to be touched in some way by the warmth it radiates.

During the interview Sister Frances spoke of her life as a novice and a nun before Helen House was established. She described how she learned to know God's presence and draw on his strength during her daily routine of prayer, Bible study and meditation – a life that reflected her marriage to Christ through her devotion to spending time with him. It was a God-centric way of living that taught her to extend the practice of prayer and devotion even to mundane household duties like peeling potatoes and preparing meals.

She went on to describe how God led her to found Helen House. She spoke of the hectic schedule it had involved and of how more recently God had taken her through a further busy and stressful programme of fund-raising as she established a second hospice, Douglas House. What really stuck in my mind was the fact that she attributed her energy and drive, her resilience in the face of daily tragedy and her ability to bring God's love into hurting families to the phase in her life when her main priority had been to spend time with God. It was during this time that she had learned to charge her batteries and develop the depths of relationship with God that could sustain her through her current ministry.

The yoke Jesus talks about is easy and the burden he shares with us is light.[5] When, through loving obedience to God, we discover the good works he has prepared for us we will stop burning ourselves out trying to serve

him.[6] We may no longer run the youth club or lead the
Sunday service. We may even be helping out at the local
football club instead – but if it is from God, he will bless
it and turn even the most mundane and unspiritual of
activities into an experience through which we grow in
joy, peace and love. When our works are inspired by
God they will radiate his love. Only then will we truly
be salt and light in the world and our actions flavour the
society we live in.

> *"The God who made the world and everything in it is the Lord*
> *of heaven and earth and does not live in temples built by*
> *hands. And he is not served by human hands, as if he needed*
> *anything, because he himself gives all men life and breath and*
> *everything else."*
>
> Acts 17:24-25

Beyond the fringe

It was during Mission England in the 1980s that I think
the rot of disillusionment began to gain a real foothold
in my Christian life. This was a nationwide programme
of evangelism that used a series of Billy Graham rallies
as a centrepiece for locally initiated activity in towns and
cities across the country. Although we were perhaps a
little sceptical about how Billy Graham would be
received by young people, a number of youth leaders in
our town agreed to work together on a programme of
creative activity in schools and town halls and on the
streets. We formed music, dance and drama groups,
invited speakers and organized concerts at local venues.

It was a massive amount of work driven by a handful
of dedicated young people from churches across the
town, but it was fun, it was making an impact and it

looked like a project with a long-term future: at least it did until one of the more ambitious local ministers decided to intervene. In our naivety we had given no serious thought to how the 'fruits' from our activity would be divided amongst the different churches: it wasn't really an issue for us because people would simply go to the church of the friend that invited them to an event, or the one nearest their home. But this minister wanted his cut and was prepared to fight for it. Nearing exhaustion from my work on the project, I simply did not have the mental energy for the massive disagreement that ensued, nor for the division that it caused amongst leaders which culminated in some withdrawing their young people from the activity. It totally devalued what we were trying to achieve and brought to mind the soldiers casting lots over Christ's clothing as he hung on the cross. It marked the beginning of the end for the project and I took one of my first steps on the road to the fringe.

I have often wondered if things could have ended differently. If it hadn't been 'my project', would I have felt personally under attack? If the minister concerned had put people's experience of God before fodder for his pews, would he have attacked in the first place? If my relationship with God had been my primary motivation, would I have pushed myself so hard, and would I have ended up nursing my anger and disappointment on my way to the fringe? It has taken me another twenty years to learn that unless knowing and following God's heart is my primary objective, anything I turn my hand to in God's name is unlikely to produce fruit and may well result in strife and hurt.

In his admonition of Israel, the prophet Malachi accuses people of robbing God by failing to give him the full tithe.[7] It wasn't because they weren't giving; they

had got the message wrong and allowed their ritual giving to replace their relationship with God. Tithing and
sacrifice had become a duty, a cultural requirement,
something to launder their guilty consciences, something that without the energy of relationship became so
half-hearted it was odious to God. He did not need their
sacrifice or their money; he wanted gifts motivated by
love, obedience and faith. If our spiritual harvest has
failed we need to examine our offering. We must look at
all our activity and, if our labours have ended in disappointment or if we have burned ourselves out trying to
keep the ship of our churches afloat, we must have the
courage to step back and measure our motivation
against the benchmark of God's love – and ask if we
have yoked ourselves to our churches rather than to
Christ.

There is something about human nature that wants –
perhaps even needs – to work. When tempered by love
this produces in us the type of service that Jesus demon-
strated in washing the disciples' feet.[8] On the one hand
it was a tremendous act of humility, but on the other, an
act of intimacy that expressed deep love and provided a
pattern for relationships that was to become the foundation of the early church. Paul used the image of the body
to portray the same concept of relational service – every
organ closely knitted together and each part humbly fulfilling a God-given role that, only in conjunction with
the other parts, allows the body as a whole to function.[9]
Each member quietly and often invisibly serving the
other; no one working in isolation, all in subjection to
each other and the head.

God meant his church to be like a finely tuned organ-
ism through which love can flow and grow – a mechanism with nothing quite like it for creating a sense of
belonging, self-worth and wholeness. If our primary

concern is our identity, what part of the body we are rather than the fact that we are part of it; if we are too busy trying to create a role rather than finding the role we are given, or if we are competing with others for recognition, it will produce something more akin to the pain-ridden, dysfunctional body of an aged arthritic than the dynamic bride of Christ. Our emphasis on role rather than relationship excludes us from the body and excludes Christ from his church.

If we start with the relationship and, as individuals and churches, withdraw from our busy programmes for a while and sit at the feet of Jesus, we will find the role that allows us to function as a body. If we are to bear the lasting fruit God has appointed, we need a 'fast' when we feed our souls on time spent with God rather than in service.[10] If we take just a little time out to establish what he has planned for us, we will be surprised at how productive our lives can suddenly become when we put our hands to the plough again.

A farmer in the Bavarian village where we once lived decided to sell up and purchase a massive ranch in Canada. His family had three generations of farming experience, so he thought he knew his stuff, and for a number of years he planted thousands of hectares of wheat because that is what he believed one grew in Canada. After several poor harvests he eventually got an expert opinion on his soil and the local climate. The results showed that it was not really suitable for wheat but ideal for cattle. On this advice he changed to beef production and was profitable within a very short time.

When our activity fails to produce the fruit we had hoped for, it is much easier just to keep busy, to work harder, be more innovative – to leave the faithful workers to collect their own straw as they make the bricks of the church they are serving.[11] We may have experienced several years with poor yields, labouring for produce that just won't grow. But after examining the soil of our hearts in God's presence and investing our energy in the crop he has prepared for us, we will enter a season of blessing and find a harvest of fruitfulness we never thought possible.

To the point

- Do you labour under an unnecessary burden of 'service' when God's primary expectation of you is that you seek to know and love him?
- To what extent is your 'service' motivated by fear of rejection, desire for recognition or a guilty conscience?
- Have you discovered the joy of 'service' motivated by a love for God?
- Are you really serving God or are you labouring for your church?
- Do your good works encourage a growing and fruitful relationship with God or do they leave you with insufficient time to spend with him?
- Is your self-esteem based on successful works?
- Is your disappointment with God in reality a disappointment with people's response to your service?
- Are you missing the blessing God is offering you through your relationships because you are looking for blessings through your works?
- Do you have the courage to cancel your activity for a while and sit at the feet of Jesus?

Meditation

The parable of the workers in the vineyard

"For the Kingdom of Heaven is like a landowner who went out early in the morning to hire men to work in his vineyard. He agreed to pay them a denarius for the day and sent them into his vineyard.

"About the third hour he went out and saw others standing in the market-place doing nothing. He told them, 'You also go and work in my vineyard, and I will pay you whatever is right.' So they went.

"He went out again about the sixth hour and the ninth hour and did the same thing. About the eleventh hour he went out and found still others standing around. He asked them, 'Why have you been standing here all day long doing nothing?'

"'Because no-one has hired us,' they answered. "*He said to them, 'You also go and work in my vineyard.'*

"When evening came, the owner of the vineyard said to the foreman, 'Call the workers and pay them their wages, beginning with the last ones hired and going on to the first.'

"The workers who were hired about the eleventh hour came and each received a denarius. So when those came who were hired first, they expected to receive more. But each one of them also received a denarius. When they received it, they began to grumble against the landowner. 'These men who were hired last worked only one hour,' they said, 'and you have made them equal to us who have borne the burden of the work and the heat of the day.'

"But he answered one of them, 'Friend, I am not being unfair to you. Didn't you agree to work for a denarius? Take your pay and go. I want to give the man who was hired last the same as I gave you. Don't I have the right to do what I want with my own money? Or are you envious because I am generous?

"So the last will be first, and the first will be last."
Matthew 20:1-16

- In our enthusiasm to work we might push to the front of the queue or work harder than all our colleagues, but God is not measuring us on performance: we might find ourselves at the back of the queue when it comes to a reward.
- From this parable it is clear that God places a different value on work than we do. He seems to regard the invitation to enter the vineyard and participate in the harvest with him as part of the reward.
- If, in our service, our incentive is a reward that can be measured in human terms such as recognition by fellow Christians or numerical growth in church membership, we will be disappointed. If, however, our primary motivation is simply to please the master of the harvest, we will discover a far greater reward than we expected.
- God deals with each of us as individuals. If we compare our work with that of others we will always find somebody who appears, in human terms, to get a greater reward for doing less work.
- Envy and jealousy will rob us of our reward and blind us to God's generosity. If we are preoccupied with the blessings of others we will not see the value of our own work.
- When we understand the extent of God's kindness to us we may realize that even if in human terms we feel we have been treated unfairly, in heavenly terms we have more than we could ever wish for.
- When we understand the heart of the master we will share in the joy of his generosity to others.

"I hate, I despise your religious feasts; I cannot stand your religious assemblies. Even though you bring me burnt

offerings and grain offerings, I will not accept them. Though you bring choice fellowship offerings, I will have no regard for them. Away with the noise of your songs! I will not listen to the music of your harps. But let justice roll on like a river, righteousness like a never-failing stream!"

Amos 5:21-24

Keep on loving each other as brothers. Do not forget to entertain strangers, for by so doing some people have entertained angels without knowing it.

Hebrews 13:1-2

"For I desire mercy, not sacrifice, and acknowledgement of God rather than burnt offerings."

Hosea 6:6

Prayer

Teach me, Lord, the simple yet pure joy of spending time with you. Help me, Lord, to make obedience my highest priority and love my highest goal. Show me the works that you have prepared for me and don't let me be distracted by works that I would try to prepare for you. Amen.

Notes

[1] Eph. 4:16.
[2] Mt. 4:10.
[3] Mich. 6:8.
[4] Lk. 10:38-42.
[5] Mt. 11:29-30.
[6] Eph. 2:10.

7 Mal. 3:8-12.
8 Jn. 13:4-7.
9 1 Cor. 12:12-31.
10 Jn. 15:16.
11 Gen. 5:6-8.

The sixty minute child

"So do not worry, saying, 'What shall we eat?' or 'What shall we drink?' or 'What shall we wear?' For the pagans run after all these things, and your heavenly Father knows that you need them. But seek first his kingdom and his righteousness, and all these things will be given to you as well."

Matthew 6:31-33

A couple of years ago I arrived home from work one day to find a note on my pillow from my son who was 6 at the time. Instead of one of his friendly little notes to tell me he loved me, this one contained just four words: 'I hate you, Dad.' It wasn't the words that got to me: I knew he didn't really hate me. It was the anger and the pain in that short sentence that took my breath away. Like a punch in the stomach, it left me dazed and winded. I believed we had a close relationship, but at the time I was stressed out with long hours at work, travelling, and a struggle to keep my employer happy whilst managing a health problem that, in itself, left me exhausted. Although I spent time with the family my mind was usually somewhere else. I was always busy, always rushing, and it had reached the point where I frequently didn't even have the patience to let my son finish a sentence when he tried to talk to me. As painful as it was, I was grateful for his note. Through my neglect my relationship with him was seriously under threat, but I had been too busy even to notice.

In the majority of failed relationships it is not the big issues that cause the breakdown but run-of-the-mill things. It may take a serious problem to add the final straw, but generally it is the daily pressures and stresses like work and money that wear down the bonds we share with the people we love. These things have nothing inherently wrong with them, but when they fill our lives and prevent us communicating they can rob us of intimacy and love and wash away the foundations that hold us together.

I have often wondered why nobody ever got round to forming Workaholics Anonymous – until recently, that is, when I discovered that somebody had. In the past I have looked down on friends and colleagues who appear to put their job before their families and other people-oriented activity. It wasn't until ill health finally rendered me unable to work all the hours God sent that I realized they were probably no more aware of their addiction to work than I had been to mine. Of course it wasn't just work – I wanted to be the best dad and the best husband as well – but that is probably the same for most of us. I don't really know how it happened, but in spite of all my high ideals as a young person, I had subscribed to a system that was slowly but surely eating away at all the things that were of value to me. Like any form of dependency, my addiction to work and all that goes with it was squeezing out my family and friends. Looking back over the years, I can see how it also filled the vacuum in my life that I had been unable to fill in church. In fact, although I can come up with many reasons for my life at the fringe, the main reason that I remained there for so long was not so much spiritual crisis but simply that I was too busy to think about anything other than my material day-to-day existence.

The time we spend with God is vital to growing our relationship with him. But in a society where time is considered our most valuable asset, it is often here more than anywhere else that we find ourselves fighting a losing battle. In his book *The Sixty Minute Father*, Rob Parsons talks about the need to take time for our children if we are to have a functional relationship with them. The same issue of time is highlighted in his book *The Sixty Minute Marriage*. In both cases he discusses the power of our work-driven lives to kill communication, to prevent young relationships maturing, and to erode established ones. I chose 'The sixty minute child' as the title for this chapter because we face the same challenge if, as children of God, we want to develop a genuine, growing relationship with the Father – or for that matter with his people.

Statistics tell us that, on average, in the UK we work some of the longest hours in Europe.[1] Having travelled quite extensively on business, I am convinced that in many industries across the world we are spending ridiculous amounts of time at the office or factory. We have created a labour culture where we are expected to work long days and demonstrate our commitment to our employers by our contempt for any work-time directives our governments half-heartedly produce. We travel long distances to and from our place of work and many of us are required to spend extended periods of time away from home. If we work in lower-paid jobs, we often have to clock up overtime or take on a second job to get by. In many areas the cost of living is so high that the option of a partner staying at home to look after the kids is a luxury only a few can afford.

When we get home of an evening, we are usually too tired to do much more than watch the television or read a book, and our weekends are consumed by the DIY projects we need to undertake in order to keep the house and garden in shape. Occasionally we make time for friends, but it is increasingly difficult to find enough time to penetrate our safety barriers of superficiality and build lasting relationships. Even the traditional pint and a chat at the pub seem to have been replaced by large-screen televisions and live sports coverage. Relationships become a duty and a strain, and it is hardly surprising that church can become an additional pressure that we could do without, especially if we feel we ought to be engaged in church activity.

Eventually many of us even begin to resent the hold church has on our consciences. We have no time to digest any in-depth teaching and our pastors have little choice but to serve up soundbite sermons and fast-food religion. Our times of private devotion, when we have them, are rarely more than somebody else's blessed thoughts prepared for us like a microwave dinner. God on the go for the twenty-first-century believer – not the way that most church leaders or authors of Bible notes would like it, but increasingly the only way to get a message over. In practice, our leaders are usually just as busy as the rest of us and suffering the same stress-related illnesses that are becoming the plague of contemporary society.

When we don't even have time for people, the last thing we have time for is a relationship with God. For most of us it seems increasingly difficult to find opportunity for anything more than keeping the roof over our heads and maintaining our family lives, but if we want to revitalize our Christian lives we must take time to seek God. Not time for more activity in the church, not even time to attend more services, meetings, or conferences, but quality time with our God – and not just quality but quantity as well, because, as with our partners and our children, we can't develop and maintain a relationship on fifteen minutes a day.

If we are honest, though, most of us get a buzz out of our hard work. It is great for our self-esteem when a project succeeds and even better if it leads to our promotion. We get an adrenaline rush when a deal comes off and we live for the high of the long and frantic hours and endless cups of coffee when a task is particularly challenging. Like other men, I moan to my wife about business trips, I genuinely miss the family terribly when I travel and I get tired out hanging around airport lounges and hotel lobbies. I nonetheless love being away and enjoy the thrill of visiting new cities and learning about new cultures, even though most of what I see is from a taxi or a conference hall. There is something about being on the road again – if I stay at home for more than a few weeks I start to get irritable and long for the freedom and independence of the airport departure lounge and a cosy hotel room in some far-flung corner of the world.

It is great if we enjoy our work – we are very privileged if we find what we do interesting and rewarding. The problem is that we often become emotionally and psychologically job-dependent. It becomes the critical factor in our self-esteem and identity, and in so doing it takes the place of God and our loved ones. We are self-sufficient and don't register our need of God; we live our lives at such a tremendous speed that we don't even notice there's a problem until a wheel comes off. Then we wonder why we are getting divorced or why the kids don't speak to us any more, why we are washed up at the fringes of church life and why our faith has lost its vitality.

For those who feel they are only trying to make ends meet, my depiction of contemporary working patterns might sound exaggerated. When we take a close and honest look at our lives, though, is that really all we are doing? If things were suddenly to crash, would we look back on our short-lived successes and fleeting feel-good moments as wise investments of our transitory lives? Or would we feel cheated, let down, used? To say we are being conned would be unfair, because most of the time we get a great deal of pleasure out of our work and the standard of living our job allows us. Is it possible, though, that some of the things our standard of living offers are only satisfying because we have bought in to a culture that tells us that this is the way to enjoy life – a culture that we have substituted for the deeper, more valuable things that are missing in our faith and our relationships?

The problem is not simply the hours we work. If we are not being led by our love and our search for God, we are being driven by the values we have absorbed from the society around us. We take the same values that underpin our businesses and our market economies into our homes and our churches. We subscribe to a system that makes everything a commodity, from products to people, and although we have given everything a price we have removed its value in the process. We are dedicated to our employers but when push comes to shove, they are bound by their dedication to delivering share-holder value. We are bombarded from dawn till dusk by marketing for things 'we can't live without' and become ensnared in a vicious cycle of consumerism that we fear to break in case we can't get back in again – a cycle that fuels a cruel competition between the haves and have-mores and turns the lives of the vulnerable have-nots into a nightmare of slavery to work and debt. Although we may all at times feel imprisoned by the pressures and expectations of trying to keep pace with modern lifestyles, we don't have the courage to break free. It may well be easier for a camel to pass through the eye of a needle than for many of us to find the time to really get to know the God we say we believe in.

The world of commerce has invented a very clever mechanism that is designed to ensure we are permanently discontented – not so much that we notice it but just enough to make sure we don't stop buying. It exploits our innate need for contentment and happiness by constantly redefining the ingredients of a fulfilled and enjoyable life. For most of us this is a mild, almost subconscious phenomenon, but it keeps us redecorating our living rooms once a year and staying at the office until the boss – also a victim of the same philosophy and also working late – has seen that we are still at our computers when he goes home. For those who really do have to struggle to feed and clothe their children it has all the potential to make life a living hell of worry and despair. On Sunday we sing of our freedom in Christ, but is this yet another Christian cliché? Is it something that we conveniently interpret in spiritual terms to avoid acknowledging to ourselves that on Monday we return to the shackles of our daily routines and the lifestyles to which we are bound?

We have so many people in our society who are extremely well off and so many affluent celebrities as role models. Consequently, when we read the story of Jesus' conversation with a rich young man, we don't recognize the relevance of his warning about the grip of wealth because we don't think of ourselves as being rich.[2] Most of us are rich, even if we are not well off by western standards, and maintaining our riches has become a top priority in our lives – usually to the exclusion of anything spiritual. We may be too busy to really live, but we have become used to our standard of living, and if we fear we can't maintain it, we shed blood, sweat and tears, we lose sleep and finally make ourselves unwell trying to protect it.

The term greed sounds hard, but *The Concise Oxford Dictionary* defines it simply as excessive desire. This is what our consumer society has done for us: it has created in us an excessive desire that has become like an illness that harms everybody it touches – especially the weak and the vulnerable. As long as we don't recognize and acknowledge it for what it is, we will be unable to see that slavery to this excessive desire is at the root of many of our problems, especially the frustration and fruitlessness in our Christian life. We will also remain blind to the damage it is causing to relationships, people and the environment across the whole of the global community – the price that we all, but particularly the poor, are paying for our lifestyles.

We might believe that we are struggling to make ends meet – and for many even in the rich West this is truly the case – but the majority of us are just maintaining a lifestyle with an expanding waistline that is constantly pushing the two ends farther apart. In our minds we may have separated world poverty from our daily experience of God, but the developing world hasn't – and it is no wonder that western Christians are regarded by many adherents of other faiths as the cause of the poverty and injustices they suffer.

It is only when we learn to love that we can recognize, in more than just our intellect, the horrific poverty and suffering that we witness on our television screens and in our newspapers. The knowledge is there, but hermetically sealed in a compartment of its own so that the smell cannot touch our lifestyles. We may not be rich when we look at the people we live, work and go to church with, but against the backdrop of the world's suffering it is easy to see why greed is singled out in the Bible as a particularly evil form of idolatry.[3] It is very telling that over the centuries the church has become obsessed with sexual sin and failed to read the rest of the verse that puts greed into the same bag. We preach that sexual immorality defiles the temple of our bodies but forget that if we allow greed to creep in where love should be, our enslaved lives defile the whole of the church and the world around it.

It isn't usually until we are unable to compete in the race, unable to deliver and failing to meet expectations, that we realize just what a trap we are in, and how the so-called Protestant work ethic that underpins many of our western principles has made us slaves to a system where hard work and productivity become the measure of our value. However, when our marriage breaks up or our teenager starts taking drugs, we see through it, and the mirage of our lifestyle shimmers and disappears. If only the impact this lifestyle is having on our faith were as obvious!

When I look back over the years I have spent at the fringe, I must acknowledge that I have been far too busy to give much serious thought to my relationship with God. An occasional twinge of guilt perhaps, because I haven't been to church or read my Bible, but how often, during this period, did I take the time to be still and meditate on things of God? I may have called out to him in anger or at times of crisis, but I never sought to know him or even took the time to listen for a reply. Why? Because I was working all the hours God sent in a futile attempt to prove that I do make the grade, that I am worth a lot more than I am paid and all the other things that drive us onwards and upwards in our jobs. In a world without fixed boundaries we are constantly striving towards some imaginary standard. It is only when God's love gives us a real standard that we can truly be free – free to enjoy our relationship with our loved ones and free to enjoy a relationship with God and his people.

Some of us arrive at the fringe because of the values we allow to enslave us, and others become slaves to these values because of the void that drove them to the fringe. Either way we become accustomed to a comfortable lifestyle that makes it very difficult to turn to God. The voice of our hurts and disappointments masks the niggling voice of our spiritual hunger and our conscience and provides us with an excellent excuse for staying put. Like many enthusiastic young Christians in the UK, I once wrestled with the question of where the dividing line lies between too much and enough. I had struggled with the dilemma of having so much whilst being aware of the terrible poverty and exclusion around me, and I deliberated over the frustration of being unable to make a significant difference. It wasn't career ambitions or a desire for nice things that drove me to the fringe, but it didn't take me long to unwittingly acquire these traits and to hold on to them tightly as the love that had once inspired me cooled. It is amazing how effectively the modern comforts of middle-class mediocrity can make the things we once considered important vanish from our minds – at least for a while.

I am not trying to advocate some form of alternative minimalist lifestyle – but it is a call to get a life, to examine the values that as churches and individuals we have embraced and to be honest with ourselves about the things that separate us from God and his people. It is also an appeal for Christians to challenge the accepted norms of our society and not be afraid to conclude that things are not as they should be. It is not a declaration that holidays abroad or nice houses are inherently evil, but it is a plea to consider the real price we sometimes pay for these things. The Bible does not forbid riches and it encourages work, but it warns against the grip that our wealth and consequently our job can have on us, and the epidemic of greed that this feeds. It is this that I need to be free from. It is not having riches but seeking them that is the problem, because it precludes a search for the Kingdom of God.

A couple of years ago I sailed across the English Channel with some friends. On the return voyage I was allowed for the first time to take a four-hour watch on my own. It was a fantastic feeling. Alone at the wheel, completely in charge of the boat, with the skipper and crew asleep below – miles from land with only the sea and the stars to keep me company. I don't think I have ever felt quite so free, so at peace with myself and my environment.

The euphoria began to wear off as the fog came down and I could no longer make out the lights of the ships crossing my bows. The English Channel is one of the world's busiest shipping lanes, and the nearer I got to the coast the more ships I encountered on their way out of Southampton. In the dark and the fog they looked like giant ghost ships, but because I was unable to tell how close they were or which direction they were heading in, they were far more frightening. In my attempts to avoid them I changed direction time and time again until I was miles off course, but I was too frightened to leave the helm to go below and check the chart, and too proud to wake the crew and ask for help. As dawn finally broke over the horizon, the skipper emerged from his cabin and took the wheel. The overwhelming sense of relief as I handed over command of the vessel was so much greater than the freedom I had felt as I had taken charge just a few traumatic hours earlier.

We desire to be free but the world's definition of freedom makes us slaves to our jobs, our credit card companies, our oversized mortgages and the things we cannot have. If, however, the alternative is slavery to God, can Christians really talk of freedom? Is it that we have misunderstood what true freedom is? Something in our nature longs for independence and control over our own lives, but could it be that we only find true freedom when we submit our lives to a higher authority who has our best interests at heart? We may feel free and believe we have command of our vessel, but we will always be subject to the tides and winds of the evil in our world and our human nature – forces that will inevitably take us off a safe course and into dangerous and stressful waters, that will rob us of the joy of the voyage, and may even land us on a reef.

If I am honest, I fear to look too closely at the heart of God, because of the greed that it will expose in me and the riches I may well have to give up. But as I have acknowledged that ultimately I can never be truly in control of my life and have stepped out in search of a closer walk with God, I have found these fears are replaced by a yearning for the type of freedom that Christ offers. They give way to a longing for a freedom that is not motivated by the shallow values that control our society but by love and compassion, by things that make a difference. I have begun to see the value systems to which I have yoked myself for what they really are, and to recognize the lie of self-sufficiency. Slowly, very slowly, I am starting to learn the freedom that submission to God can really bring; why it is that the birds of the air greet us with a joyful carefree song in the morning, and why the flowers that radiate God's extravagance and beauty don't worry about the things for which until quite recently I was working myself to death.

"Therefore I tell you, do not worry about your life, what you will eat or drink; or about your body, what you will wear. Is not life more important than food, and the body more important than clothes? Look at the birds of the air; they do not sow or reap or store away in barns, and yet your heavenly Father feeds them. Are you not much more valuable than they? Who of you by worrying can add a single hour to his life?

"And why do you worry about clothes? See how the lilies of the field grow. They do not labour or spin. Yet I tell you that not even Solomon in all his splendour was dressed like one of these. If that is how God clothes the grass of the field, which is here today and tomorrow is thrown into the fire, will he not much more clothe you, O you of little faith? So do not worry, saying, 'What shall we eat?' or 'What shall we drink?' or 'What shall we wear?' For the pagans run after all these things, and your heavenly Father knows that you need them. But seek first his kingdom and his righteousness, and all these things will be given to you as well. Therefore do not worry about tomorrow, for tomorrow will worry about itself. Each day has enough trouble of its own."

Matthew 6:25-34

Beyond the fringe

Without the framework of the law of love in our lives, without Christ at the centre of our work, family and church routines, we become easy prey for idols. We unsuspectingly welcome as normal and acceptable the gods of contemporary society into our church communities, and church culture becomes little more than an extension of the world. The values that dictate our lives suppress our spiritual hunger, smother our love and extinguish the flame of our witness – our spirituality loses its meaning, and the message of the church becomes meaningless to the world. When we stop our frantic activity and peel away the band-aid of materialism, the chances are that we will find that our faith and our lives are dull, empty and unfruitful.

As Christians we are called to be different and to make a difference to our society. The Christian life is meant to be an adventure: an adventure in spirituality and in the practical expression of the love and ideals of Christ in our lives. Our youthful idealism wasn't wrong – we just tried to change the world without allowing God's love to change us. We need to rediscover the values that motivated us when we first came to Christ; we must reconfigure our priorities so that we work to live rather than living to work; we must de-clutter our lives to make room for God and we must redirect our time towards a search for intimacy with him. This might involve a radical change of direction; it will certainly require a simpler, less hectic and less crowded lifestyle. Even in human terms there is much to be gained by removing the dead wood from our daily existence, but it is essential if God is to play a genuine role in our lives; ultimately it is vital for our happiness and the happiness of our loved ones.

Often it will just mean watching a bit less television, spending fewer hours on the internet, getting up a bit earlier, decorating one room a year instead of the whole house, and making better use of the resources we already have. But if God is God, we have to begin to live as if he is, and this will mean more than just a superficial 'life-makeover'. It might mean a change of job, a drop in income, a smaller house or some other major lifestyle change. What it can't be is a time management exercise: it must be a change of master. Slaves need to be free, not to manage their time better!

A few years ago I travelled to India as part of an industry delegation conducting market research into the country's emerging biotechnology sector on behalf of the Department of Trade and Industry. It was an opportunity to go to a country I have always wished to visit and I fell in love with it before I had even reached my hotel room. Our mission involved travelling from region to region interviewing scientists and visiting leading biotech and pharmaceutical companies. It was the first time I had encountered extreme poverty, and the contrast between the plush offices and well-equipped laboratories that we visited and the desperation on their doorsteps was almost unbearable. On our way to panelled boardrooms we would drive through slums where families lived in shacks made of plastic sheets, where the lucky ones had a disused sewer pipe for a home, and where emaciated children ran behind our air-conditioned vehicles begging for a few rupees.

To be fair, the research programmes of many of the biotechnology companies I have met in India and other developing countries are not driven entirely by a commercial agenda, and some really do target the issues of disease and malnutrition amongst their poor communities. However, as I returned home to write my report I struggled for days with the fact that on a global scale so much knowledge, creativity and innovation is available in this sector, but generally, apart from some token altruism, its primary aim is to find the next biotech blockbuster rather than to address the needs of the poor and the hungry. I understood the challenges and costs of producing new drugs and the need for a return on the massive investments involved. It nonetheless brought home to me just how seriously wrong our enterprise culture has so many of its priorities, and just how different the world would be if even only 10 per cent of our cutting edge capabilities were used for the things that matter to God.

Like our ability to love, our creativity and enterprise are characteristics we have in common with God. There is something of an entrepreneur in all of us, and the church has so much to offer when we shake off the world's values and make the priorities of Christ our motivation. Where our values have been influenced by the world, tithing, charity and good works frequently become just another part of our Christian duty – little more than a mechanism for a clean conscience or even part of a quid pro quo deal with God that underpins our desire for material blessing. However, in the context of love, big-heartedness – or God-heartedness – can offer us a route out of bondage to our work culture and into the culture of Christ. I believe that if we are willing to listen to God's heart and learn love-driven giving, not just of our money but of our time, our gifts, our affection and our lives, we will find that he offers each of us an adventure, an invitation to new levels of freedom and joy.

God is calling his people to swim against the tide of our greed-driven culture, to be entrepreneurial in the way we use our abilities and resources to tackle society's challenges. A closer walk with God may not lead us to the impoverished shanty towns of the developing world, but we will begin to recognize the poor and oppressed, the widows and orphans on our own doorsteps and in our churches. The step God requires of us might be to give up our jobs and work with the deprived at the margins of society or it could simply be to spend more time in prayer for our grandchildren or enjoying our loved ones. But as we do step out to follow the culture of Christ, when we challenge society's values and risk being different, he will not only take us beyond the mediocrity of our lives at the fringes of our churches but he will use us to impact the lives of the people around us.

To the point

- Do you find yourself in a spiritual desert because you have buried your head in the sand of busy working patterns?
- Have you found the freedom in your work situation that comes when your self-esteem is based on your knowledge of God's love for you?
- Is your reliance on contemporary comforts robbing you of a deep and long-lasting comfort that comes from closeness to God?
- Do you sometimes feel tempted to turn to shopping or eating for comfort?
- Have you discovered the joy that you can have in your daily life and work when you let God do the worrying?
- Do you know the peace that can accompany you through the day when you start it with time spent in quiet prayer and meditation?
- Are you willing to make changes in the way you live if this allows you to move beyond the spiritual fringe and closer to the heart of God?
- Are you willing to risk an adventure in life by allowing love to dictate your living and working patterns?

Meditation

The parable of the wedding banquet

> *Jesus spoke to them again in parables, saying: "The kingdom of heaven is like a king who prepared a wedding banquet for his son. He sent his servants to those who had been invited to the banquet to tell them to come, but they refused to come.*

"Then he sent some more servants and said, 'Tell those who have been invited that I have prepared my dinner: My oxen and fattened cattle have been slaughtered, and everything is ready. Come to the wedding banquet.'

"But they paid no attention and went off – one to his field, another to his business. The rest seized his servants, ill-treated them and killed them. The king was enraged. He sent his army and destroyed those murderers and burned their city.

"Then he said to his servants, 'The wedding banquet is ready, but those I invited did not deserve to come. Go to the street corners and invite to the banquet anyone you find.' So the servants went out into the streets and gathered all the people they could find, both good and bad, and the wedding hall was filled with guests.

"But when the king came in to see the guests, he noticed a man there who was not wearing wedding clothes. 'Friend,' he asked, 'how did you get in here without wedding clothes?' The man was speechless.

"Then the king told the attendants, 'Tie him hand and foot, and throw him outside, into the darkness, where there will be weeping and gnashing of teeth.'

"For many are invited, but few are chosen."

Matthew 22:1-14

The people invited to the wedding can be divided into three groups:

1. **Those who didn't know the king**. They knew something about him, and some possibly paid lip-service to the fact that he was their king, but they weren't aware of the true importance of a royal summons – or the intensity of the king's wrath towards those who refused him. In the business world we are invited to numerous parties and networking events. Often invitations just land in the bin unread because we don't

have time to sort out the ones that might be useful. We are bombarded with annoying, unsolicited spam and in our stress many of us have discarded important documents that have been caught up in a volley of junk mail. If our spiritual life is a disappointment, perhaps we have been too busy to distinguish the call of the king from the call of the world. If we wish to know him properly, we need to slow down sufficiently to have time to recognize, read and respond to his invitations.

2. **Those who thought they knew the king**. The parable brings to mind a wonderful German expression that means 'to dance at two weddings at the same time'. Basically it means that we want to have our cake and eat it – we want the best of both worlds. One of the guests had been busy working but had managed to squeeze the king's party in between meetings. Unfortunately he had forgotten to change into his wedding clothes – which was fine until the king arrived and had him thrown out. Of course he was speechless: he had, after all, juggled his hectic schedule to make room for the king and was pleased with himself for balancing things so well. We may be proud that we manage to make room for God in our chaotic lives, but if he is just another item on a long to-do list we shouldn't be surprised to find he can't make room for us at his son's wedding banquet.

3. **Those who knew the king**. We all envy people who seem to lead a carefree existence, who can afford time to entertain and go to parties. Those who know the king will also know that his priorities are different to ours, that he regards relationships with him, with friends and family, with fellow Christians as far more important than our work. Those who risk living according to his priorities enjoy the freedom of knowing a king who will

make sure that they lack nothing. They can afford to respond to his invitation and live by his values without fear.

When we first heard this parable at Sunday school or during our early days in the church, we probably felt certain about which category we belonged to. If, however, we have allowed our busy lives to take over, could this have changed? For those of us who are willing to accept the invitation and leave our work for a while, the party has already started – we just need to make sure we are dressed appropriately when the king arrives.

> *"Do not work for food that spoils, but for food that endures to eternal life, which the Son of Man will give you. On him God the Father has placed his seal of approval." Then they asked him, "What must we do to do the works God requires?" Jesus answered, "The work of God is this: to believe in the one he has sent."*
>
> John 6:27-29

> *"Do not store up for yourselves treasures on earth, where moth and rust destroy, and where thieves break in and steal. But store up for yourselves treasures in heaven, where moth and rust do not destroy, and where thieves do not break in and steal. For where your treasure is, there your heart will be also."*
>
> Matthew 6:19-21

> *Cast all your anxiety on him because he cares for you.*
>
> 1 Peter 5:7

Prayer

Open my eyes, Lord, to the things that enslave me. Forgive me because I have bought in to a system that is often based on standards that are contrary to the things you have taught. Help me to walk in your footsteps and to recognize and reject the selfishness and greed of our culture. Help me to seek my riches only in your love, and my fulfilment through obedience to you. Amen.

Notes

1. Chartered Institute of Personnel and Development, June 2005.
2. Mt. 19:16-24.
3. Eph. 5:5.

8

Faith, hope and love

There is no fear in love. But perfect love drives out fear,
because fear has to do with punishment. The one who fears is
not made perfect in love.

1 John 4:18

The unfaithfulness of the Children of Israel seems so
obvious to us that we find it hard to believe they could be
so foolish. As I have begun to recognize and acknowledge my own unfaithfulness, I have come to understand
that when we look beyond our outward actions there is
often a common root linking much of our modern infidelity to theirs, namely fear.

Though not sinful in itself, fear is an insidious emotion
that can eat away at our soul and lead us to compromise
our relationship with God and with his people. It was
fear of the strength and the size of their enemies that left
the Israelites walking in the desert for 40 years, and fear
of being different to the neighbouring nations that made
them demand a king.[1] Fear imprisons our lives. It may
be, for most of us, an open prison with no apparent walls
or barbed wire, but it is a prison nonetheless. Though we
may not recognize it as fear, when it gets a grip on our life

it replaces freedom and joy with a tight knot in our stomachs – it rules our lives and dictates the way we run our families and our churches.

It is easy to be unaware of our own unfaithfulness to God, because in our black and white way of thinking we mistakenly regard infidelity as something clear-cut, like open betrayal and rebellion. More often than not, fear drags us into a grey area where our disloyalty results from an attempt to try to please two masters – to please people as well as God. We have all experienced the sting of rejection when a loved one has chosen to side with somebody else. The young wife who is torn between loyalty to her new husband and fear of her dominant mother; the husband who shows greater allegiance to the career he fears he could lose than to his wife; the teenager who deceives his parents because of his fear of rejection by his friends. We may not always recognize the moments when, out of fear, we have been disloyal and compromised the love we have for God or for others, but we know only too well the pain we feel when those we thought were our friends have done it to us.

Love cannot thrive in the presence of fear. Our fear of the opinions and power of others and the angst that sometimes overwhelms us when we look at our chaotic world undermine our faith and our relationship with God. Though not an idol itself, fear is at the root of most idolatry. Like the Children of Israel before us, we often find it easier to side with the opinions of the world we can see, and in so doing we neglect our relationship with the God we can't see.

Fear is one of the world's strongest motivators. It is at the core of the unrest we feel, and of the discontentment that drives us but never allows us to find satisfaction. It is fear of the boss or fear of unemployment that makes us slaves to our jobs, and fear of rejection that binds us to our service in the church. Fear is at the very heart of the rat-race: it allows people to control us and makes it hard for us to control ourselves, and it fires our greed because we fear we may lose out. We fear that we might be sidelined, no longer at the cutting edge in our work or at the centre of our church community. Fear also dictates the way we feel about ourselves and turns us into workaholics as we try to prove our worth. It is also often behind our biggest regrets when we have compromised our own integrity, and it is a thief that robs us of relationship with each other and with God. It steals our happiness and sadly it is just as prevalent in the church as it is in the world.

It is fear that causes us to create our own image of God. Like the wife who lies about her husband's job because she is embarrassed by his lack of seniority, we create a hyped up or toned down, politically correct picture of God that we feel will be acceptable to our unbelieving friends – a safe and non-threatening God who is unlikely to upset our finely balanced lives. We claim to want an all-powerful God, but because of our fear that the real God might let us down in public we weave our set of transparent, non-offensive spiritual clothing. If we make the god we worship less than the God of the Bible, how can we fail to be disappointed? Fear is a powerful venom that can paralyse our lives and our churches, a weapon of mass destruction that can smother our relationship with God and emasculate our faith. When, out of fear, we create a diminutive god, and our lives deny that he is the God he claims to be, our unfaithfulness is no different to that of Israel.

Unfaithfulness is really faithlessness. It is our inability to take God at his word, the word that promises he will take care of our lives and of the things that cause us stress and worry. We may not recognize it as this, though, because our evangelical tradition often puts faith in a box, turning it into an appendage to our relationship with God rather than a foundation stone. For many, faith has become like some sort of magical force – if you have enough of it, you will be healthy and prosperous; if you don't, you are a second-class Christian. Even the term 'living by faith' is reserved for the financial dependence of 'full-time' Christians, for the missionaries and ministers who, though usually salaried these days, are seen as having some special economic reliance on God.

In practice, fear is so much part of our daily lives that we are generally not even aware of it, nor are we aware of our need for faith on a daily basis. For most of us, faith is just the raft we cling to in a crisis when the ship of our lives begins to sink. It is then that we stamp our feet and cry in desperation and try with all our strength to believe, as if our belief will in itself bring about the rescue we need. If things don't work out, it is clearly because we don't have enough faith, so we end up feeling inferior and guilty – and this frequently turns our disappointment into cynicism. As long as we regard faith as some sort of magic wand with which we can harness God's power, we will not grow spiritually – and our lives will remain under the control of fear. While we remain under the control of fear our magic-wand faith will inevitably leave us feeling let down. This is why the world can say that our religion is just a crutch and often be quite close to the truth, because we treat it like one.

We are right to fear, but we fear the wrong things and for the wrong reasons. Fear is a God-given emotion that throughout nature saves lives, and it is an emotion that should send us running to God to save ours. God will bring some of us to the fringe of church life so that we can begin to confront our fears and learn the true meaning of faith. With all our talk of faith in the church, there is no place to be honest about our fears and we become blind to the hold that fear has on our lives. When we arrive at the margins of church life we have a tremendous opportunity to change this. We have probably let everybody down anyway, and we have no reputation to worry about any more. Consequently, honesty has a chance to raise its voice and challenge the fears that have lain dormant in the shallow grave of our religious language for so long. If we allow our fears to bring us to God, we will find that the fringe can actually be the starting point for real faith. We will find a new germ of hope that can ignite the flame of true belief and reliance on God.

It was my fear of a Godless universe that revived the hope that my childhood experience of God had been real, that the moments of intense and inexplicable joy and overwhelming love had been genuine. It was this hope that opened my eyes once again to the immense splendour of creation, the sense of awe when I look out at the stars at night or feel the power of the sea breaking over the bows of a boat. More than this, I saw the beauty of the people around me, their potential for good, even in an evil world, their creativity, their Godlikeness. This all screamed at me that there has to be more to life than my daily material existence – and I found the gentle voice of faith whispering in reply, 'There is.'

Because of my inability to write off my childhood faith as an illusion or to see life as nothing more than a tremendous accident, I called out in hope to God and pleaded that he make himself real to me. It was this hope that brought me to my knees, and an embryonic faith called out, 'If you are God, I want to know you. Not about you, not the bells and blessings of church life, but a God who is God, a God who is love.' I found that when I was honest about my fears and my faithlessness and reached out to God with the little hope I had, his response was to give me a small taste of the certainty that turns my hope into faith.[2]

In the same way that it was never meant to be a magic wand, faith was never supposed to be blind, nor was it to rely solely on the magnificence of creation as its inspiration. God's plan is that our faith should be built on the practical expression of his love for us in our daily lives – love that we experience directly through our walk with him, and love expressed through our relationships with others. When we acknowledge our fear and our faithlessness before him and seek him with all of our strength, it is his love that will touch our hearts and it is love that will banish fear and replace it with faith. That faith which has a certainty that comes from knowing we are loved by God – a mighty God who cares about our every need. When we bring our fear of others to him, fear, for example, of those who have rejected and hurt us, he will give us a love for them that overcomes fear and brings forgiveness and reconciliation. Love is the only soil in which our tiny seed of faith can grow, and true faith can only be the consequence of a loving relationship with God.

When we consciously put our faith in God, it allows him – through his response – to demonstrate his love for us. The tired phrase 'Let go and let God' could not really be further removed from the way God meant us to trust him, because for most of us what this really means is pretending the problem doesn't exist. In faith we are actively taking our lives and placing them in the hands of somebody we know, somebody we trust to have all the things that cause us to fear under control. Real faith cannot be passive, nor can it be worked up, but it can grow when we seek God with all of our hearts and cry out to him with the little faith we do have, 'I believe; help my unbelief.'

Looking back on my pre-fringe Christian experience, I suspect that what I had often mistaken for hope and faith was, in reality, little more than wishful thinking. It may have been partly due to a crowded life that didn't leave room for a relationship with God to grow, it may also have been because my faith was in the church and my Christian culture rather than in God, but I never really formed a true faith or discovered true hope. We know in theory that Christ died to make us free from being a slave to fear, but wishful thinking can never make this into a reality. It is this wishful thinking that makes us grit our teeth and try with all our strength to believe, hoping desperately that God will do what we ask. If we rely on wishful thinking we will feel let down and be disappointed, but if we have tasted the beginnings of a relationship with God, the love in our hearts will give us reason for true faith and grounds for true hope.

I have often asked myself why I have found my attempts to live a Christian life so difficult and why almost everything I have turned my hand to has been thwarted in some way, such that I have reached the point where I have despaired of my church experience. I can see now that it was, in part, to teach me the faith that I had asked God for a long time ago. I am sure I am not alone in this – that there are many who feel, as I did, as if they have never been so close to giving up their faith altogether. We have landed at the fringes of our churches because at some time, possibly a very long time ago, we asked God to teach us faith. Slowly he starts to show us just how little faith we really have. Then he allows life to strip away the things we have put our faith in. He brings us to the point where we are left with little more than the fear that this really could be everything – that after our three-score years and ten in a world full of injustice and fear there is nothing. Then, as we call to him from the depths of our hopelessness, he begins to teach us true faith.

Faith is an inseparable component of our relationship with God because it is a product of that relationship. In fearful human hope we come to him, in faith we enter into a relationship with him, and in the context of that relationship our faith grows and we discover a new and divine hope – a hope that 'does not disappoint us, because God has poured out his love into our hearts by the Holy Spirit, whom he has given us'.[3] In order to ask something of God in faith we need to know his love for us, and we can only know this when we seek him above all else and learn to trust him in the context of a relationship. Too often we are looking for signs, wonders and blessings to make our faith grow, but their effect on the people Jesus met was never long-lasting, nor will it be for us. In the context of a relationship, though, our faith can take small steps and grow as our practical experience of God's love grows in our daily life.

When we bring our frail hope to God and call out, asking that we might know him, and when little by little we spend time meditating in his presence, we begin to see indications of his hand on our lives. Coincidences happen that are too frequent to be a coincidence, we find a peace and joy that doesn't fit with our circumstances, and our fear begins to melt as we slowly grow in security and certainty that because God cares about us, we don't have to worry. With time, faith becomes a friend with whom we can look life's tragedy in the face and still be at peace because we know God is in control.

In simple, practical ways we will find the gentle hand of God leading us. Perhaps initially like a donkey with a bit and a bridle, but slowly the difference between being driven by fear and being led by faith and love can be discovered.[4] As we allow God to manage our jobs, our income, and even our teenage children, we will start to understand what Paul meant when he spoke of the freedom we have in Christ. Faith is what we have when we are sufficiently aware of God's love for us to loosen our grip on the worldly things that offer us security, the things we are clinging to in fear, and actively take the hand of a God that we know. It is then that we can take our first faltering steps from infancy towards maturity in faith.

God is mysterious, but evangelical culture has robbed him of some of his mystery. Those who talk about God as a 'mate', who make claims of familiarity without the fruits of intimacy with God in their lives, do incalculable damage to the fledgling faith of many believers, not to mention the credibility of the church. Real faith has the hallmark of the God of love stamped on it; it originates from love and its manifestation is with love. True faith does not discourage or leave others feeling inferior – it is infectious and sweeps others along in its wake. I believe I have occasionally seen lives changed by prophecies and evidence of the presence and power of God in church meetings: I would be lying to myself if I denied it. But so often we hear people giving us their take on God's will and God's nature in a way that creates a cheap model – a fairy godmother-like figure. They reduce God to something almost human – small, cuddly and easy to believe in – and claim a knowledge and experience of him that may raise their viewing figures but not their status in heaven. I want a God who transcends my ability to understand him, a God who fills me with wonder and brings me to my knees in reverence. Surely this is the God whose power we see in the life of Peter and Paul, the God whose tenderness we sense through the lives of the disciples Mary Magdalene and John – and this is the God who wants a relationship with us, the God who through his magnificence and his love casts out all fear.

If unfaithfulness is not living as if God is God, then living a faithful life is knowing him sufficiently to acknowledge him as God in all areas of our lives. It is believing that God is who he claims to be, with all the implications that this has for us. It is an invitation to another lifestyle, another dimension in which fear has no place – it is where the empty words of our church culture take on reality. Faith is about so much more than the occasional miracle; it is where we can find the satisfaction and meaning that we once chased after in our fear. Faith also brings freedom into our relationships with others by freeing us from the fear of hurt and rejection. Even when we are treated wrongly, faith will give us the strength to offer the other cheek, and the love and peace of God will enable us to bring healing into the situation.[5] Faith will allow our Christianity to make a genuine difference to our lives in a practical and demonstrable way, because it calms the storm of uncertainty in our hearts and minds and replaces it with a peace that surpasses all understanding.[6]

The God of Love is also the King of Peace, and it is peace along with love that replaces the void left by fear – a deep inner peace with ourselves and with God. He gives us a peace that takes away the need to prove ourselves and removes the fear of failure and the dread of what others think. How can we fear such things when we begin to grasp how God feels about us? This peace is also a gift that we can give to others through our love, because through our love and acceptance we take away their fears. We may be at the fringe of the church, but as we give of our peace and our love we will give and receive healing and we will be drawn close to the heart of God.

It was fear that made the first Adam hide himself from God, and it is the peace that Christ, the last Adam, brings that allows us to walk once again with God in the garden during the cool of the afternoon.[7] This time the garden is the sanctuary of our hearts, a place of inner peace where we can meet with him. It is when we take the time to meet here that the Holy Spirit will nurture our relationship with God. It is the time we spend in fellowship here that makes us impervious to life's pressures as we grow in confidence, fearlessness and peace. It is when we walk with God in the sanctuary of our hearts that he fills our lives and makes our hearts like his. His values become our values, and our concern is no longer the things that are happening in our life but how we can remain in God's love.

The book of Revelation talks of a seal being broken to release a fiery horse with a rider who has the power to take peace from the earth.[8] If we look at our society, it is not just bombs in our cities, war in Iraq or tension in the Middle East – people have no peace in their hearts. We are on a roller coaster of unrest that is getting faster and faster as we strive for greater and greater achievements in the hopeless, fruitless search for satisfaction and contentment – in the search for peace in our hearts. Our world is more fearful than ever before. There has never been so much uncertainty and such a sense that things are spinning out of control.

When church leaders take the time to wait on the Lord until they find their own inner peace and the faith to give up their reliance on busy programmes, they will be a light to their congregations and will help to guide them from a position of fear to a position of faith and hope. When as individuals we bring the embers of our hope to God and seek the loving relationship that fans the flames of our faith into life, we will find that we shine out as ambassadors of peace in this dark world – and the church will become a haven of love and security. The world's fear and insecurity are set to become greater, not less, and if we want to be 'seeker-sensitive churches' we need to find in our own lives the love, hope and peace that the world is searching for.

Beyond the fringe

When I was young I had a children's version of John Bunyan's *The Pilgrim's Progress*. It was full of colourful illustrations, some of which have left a far more lasting impression than the text. In one particularly striking picture, Christian, the story's main character, was portrayed kneeling at the cross with his immense burden of sin falling from his back and rolling away down the hill of Calvary. As Christians we bring our sins to the cross for forgiveness but we often neglect to leave our fear there too – fear that weighs us down and leaves us in bondage to sin's power. When we discover the freedom from fear that Christ intended, it is like taking off a very heavy rucksack after a long day's hike. Your feet may be blistered and your legs may ache, but as soon as the weight is taken from your shoulders you feel as light as a feather.

If we allow our fears to bring us to God, they provide him with an opportunity to demonstrate his love for us and to offer us a chance to know him better. As his love neutralizes our fear, our faith and our relationship deepen and trust becomes a way of life – we discover the value he places on us and the love that he has for us. The heavy ropes of fear that bound us are gradually replaced by a warming cloak of inner peace.

Our fears also give us an opportunity to grow in our relationships with each other. We all fear, but when we have the courage to share our fear, bondage to the fear of others can be transformed into a bond of love. I have a couple of friends who have spent much of their working lives visiting the world's political hot-spots defusing terrorist bombs. They are quiet, unassuming people with a gentle spirit, not at all what you would expect of somebody who has had to face fear in a way that most of us could never imagine. They talk with great reluctance of the gallantry awards they have received, and when they do it is always to play down their role and to emphasize the fact that they were just part of a team – all of whom had to confront their fears together, and all of whom shared the responsibility for the safety of each other.

I once asked how they managed to overcome their fears. What first struck me was that there was no attempt to deny that fear played a major role. We discussed the wave of fear they felt when the phone call came informing them of a mission, their struggle against a natural reluctance to leave their base to tackle the assignment, and the battle against a paralysing fear just before they made the long walk towards the bomb. There was no shame in their fear. Nobody felt under pressure to prove themselves, the team carried the fear together, and nobody was looked down on because everybody knew that the object of their fears was real.

Two factors played a key role in their ability to cope with their fears: confidence in their high-quality training and absolute trust in their fellow team members. Training taught them the necessary technical skills but it also taught them just how serious their task was and how justified their fears were. This laid the foundation for the trusting relationships on which the team was built – relationships that made it possible to manage their fear and use it to focus the mind on the task. It was this trust that allowed them to approach an explosive device confident that their colleagues would block any electronic attempts to detonate it and would protect them from sniper fire while they disabled it. They all knew the consequences of a mistake, of an error of judgement, and they all confronted their fears as a team.

Our lives and our churches would be revolutionized if we allowed love and faith to disarm our fears. When we begin to accept each other with our fears and weaknesses, we will be able to accept ourselves. When we acknowledge that we all struggle with doubts and fears, when we learn to face our fears as a family, we will no longer be enslaved to the opinions of others and no longer driven by the need to prove ourselves. Instead we will discover a fearlessness that will illuminate our families, our places of work and our communities with love, hope and peace. Courage is not a lack of fear, it is the ability to overcome fear – and this is best achieved when we grow together in love and faith.

To the point

- Have you discovered how much easier it is to walk with God when you allow him to take away your fears?
- Have you found the freedom that you can have in relationships when they are not tarnished by fear?
- Is faith part of your daily experience, or something you hope you have enough of if your worst fears are realized?

- If your faith has failed to grow, is it because you have sought growth through signs and wonders rather than by seeking the heart of God?
- Have you discovered the joy of hope and faith or do you struggle on with fearful, wishful thinking?
- Have you tasted the sense of relief that comes to all areas of your life when you are no longer driven by fear of failure?

Meditation

The parable of the wise and foolish builders

> *"Therefore everyone who hears these words of mine and puts them into practice is like a wise man who built his house on the rock. The rain came down, the streams rose, and the winds blew and beat against that house; yet it did not fall, because it had its foundation on the rock. But everyone who hears these words of mine and does not put them into practice is like a foolish man who built his house on sand. The rain came down, the streams rose, and the winds blew and beat against that house, and it fell with a great crash."*
>
> Matthew 7:24-27

- Do we ever think about what building on the rock really means? It is to build on the faith, hope and love that come from an obedient and intimate relationship with God.
- To build on the sand is to build on wishful thinking and fear.
- Everything in our culture tells us to build our house on fear, always to think of the worst-case scenario and prepare for it. A good education means a good and secure job, which means a solid financial base. We

invest, we insure, and none of it offers us the least bit of security if the worst-case scenario actually happens. Nothing can beat taking out a life insurance policy for making us think of death.

- The house built on fear is a house of stress and strife, a place where relationships struggle in a battle to survive. It is a house that feels free when the weather is good, but it becomes a prison when the walls collapse around us.

- The house built on faith and obedience stands firm on the foundation of God's love for us. Faith does not exclude common sense precautions, but it does not rely on them. Faith, like love, is entrepreneurial – it likes an adventure and takes a risk, and then finds there was no risk at all.

- The house built on faith is secure in the knowledge that a loving God will provide – a God who knows our every need. It is a house where love and peace live, a house of freedom whose walls of love provide security and shelter when the pillars of the world are crumbling.

- If, as living stones, we share each other's burden of fear and doubt, the house of God will be built into a temple of hope, faith and love.

> *Therefore let everyone who is godly pray to you while you may be found; surely when the mighty waters rise, they will not reach him. You are my hiding-place; you will protect me from trouble and surround me with songs of deliverance.*
>
> Psalm 32:6-7

> *Some trust in chariots and some in horses, but we trust in the name of the Lord our God.*
>
> Psalm 20:7

Fear of man will prove to be a snare, but whoever trusts in the Lord is kept safe.

Proverbs 29:25

Then Saul said to Samuel, "I have sinned. I violated the Lord's command and your instructions. I was afraid of the people and so I gave in to them. Now I beg you, forgive my sin and come back with me, so that I may worship the Lord." But Samuel said to him, "I will not go back with you. You have rejected the word of the Lord, and the Lord has rejected you as king over Israel!"

1 Samuel 15:24-26

Prayer

Forgive me, Father, because I often give in to my fear of the opinions of others and seek to please those around me before you. Forgive me too, Lord, for the times when my lovelessness has caused others to fear. I confess that I have not taken the time to learn to know and trust you. Teach me the security that comes from true faith, the joy that comes from hope and the freedom and courage that come from love. Amen.

Notes

1. Num. 13:26-33, 1 Sam. 8:19-20.
2. Heb. 11:1.
3. Rom. 5:5.
4. Ps. 32:8-10.
5. Lk. 6:27-30.
6. Phil. 4:7.
7. 1 Cor. 15:45-50, Gen. 3:8.
8. Rev. 6:3-4.

9

The Father's discipline?

"Because of the increase of wickedness, the love of most will grow cold . . ."

Matthew 24:12

Had this book continued the way I had originally planned it – an angry and cynical knock at the church – I am sure it would have found plenty of sympathetic readers, possibly more than it will in its final form. But I have found that as I raised my voice to shout at God about the state of the church, he has shown me the state of my heart. Where I have shown him my anger he has revealed to me his love – his love for me and the love he has for his church. Instead of the confirmation I had sought, I found myself looking into the eyes of the good shepherd. He has started, very gently, to take away the anger, the frustration and the hurt that I have laid at his feet and to lead me into the fold of his love.

The route I have travelled from being a motivated young Christian to becoming a spiritual down-and-out at the fringes of the church has been long and, at times, painful. On the way I have seen the underbelly of church life, my second-hand assumptions about God have been challenged and the filthy rags of my religious-culture-based beliefs have been torn away. God has also shown me the darkness that lurks in my own heart, the shallowness of my love and the brute beast that is my own nature when bitterness takes hold of my soul.[1]

Looking back from where I am now, I can see the hand of God on my life. I see the clear pattern of his discipline, which has hedged me in and dragged me to the point where I have had to concede my lack and my need of him. Had my disillusionment and disappointment not forced me to stop my frantic activity in the church, I would probably never have thought about whether or not God was really to be found in all the hustle and bustle of a busy Christian life. If my 'service' had not been frustrated I would not have taken my eyes off the church and looked into the eyes of God. Perhaps it is dangerous to apply my personal experience to the broader situation of the church, but having tasted again just a little of the love that for so long had been missing, and discovering the healing that the first tentative steps towards loving brings, I think it is worth the risk. I have met so many people on a similar journey to my own that I find it hard to believe a change in the hearts of the people at the fringe could fail to bring about a massive, positive change in the church.

When we take the time to stop and think about it, we all want our experience of God to be real. Whether we have retired to the margins or are still in the thick of church activity, something in us longs to see the power of God at work demonstratively in our lives, in the church and in the world. However, in spite of the untiring commitment of some Christians to pray for revival, the heavens remain silent. If we are confident that the God we know is God, surely this must make us pause and question why he has withheld the rain and the dew of his blessing from our lives and from our churches – why the very existence of the church in the west now appears to be under threat.

Could it be that in our search for clever explanations and imaginative solutions we are missing the point? Could it be that it is not the secularization of society that is causing the church's decline but a subtle secularization of the church? Is what we are experiencing as individuals and as a church in fact the Lord's discipline? Might it be that the well thought-out theories we construct to account for the famine in our land are blinding us to the truth that our labours remain fruitless because of our lukewarm love and our tepid relationships? Are the foundations of the church in fact being shaken because of the coldness and hardness of the stones out of which it is built? Have we followed our unfaithful hearts and unwittingly bowed our knee to the gods of the nations around us? Is God allowing his church to drift further and further into a spiritual wilderness, beyond the margins of society, in order to strip away some of the layers of Christian culture which, though they may reflect centuries of church tradition, have little to do with the heart of Christ?

The people of Israel had made the temple the centre of their faith. They had built a culture around it so complex and yet so far removed from what God had intended that when the Messiah, for whom they were all long-ingly waiting, finally arrived they missed him completely – and not long after they had put him to death the temple was totally destroyed and the people of Israel scattered. If God would allow the destruction of the temple in order to get Israel's attention, is it possible that he would allow the church to fall into ruin if the culture we have built around our faith has become a substitute for knowing him?

The loving, jealous God who withheld the rain for years during the time of Elijah, the God who allowed the destruction of the temple and the exile of his people in order to bring them back to him, is the same God we worship today.[2] If he is no longer at the heart of our faith, we are probably unaware that our situation is the result of our unfaithfulness. We are unlikely to recognize that our spiritual poverty is the consequence of God's discipline – discipline that in treating us as beloved children will drive us into a corner until we return to him with all our hearts.[3] If, through our lovelessness, we have grieved God's Holy Spirit, no matter how many new patches we sew onto the old cloth of our church culture, the material will continue to shrink. No amount of cosmetics and fine clothing will restore the beauty of an unfaithful bride – only a heart that reaches out in love.

I recently stood at the spot in Oxford where the reformers Hugh Latimer, Thomas Cranmer and Nicholas Ridley were burnt at the stake in the sixteenth century. I couldn't help but think of the famous words of Latimer to Ridley shortly before they died, and wonder how he would view the church of today:

'Play the man, Master Ridley; we shall this day light such a candle, by God's grace, in England, as I trust shall never be put out.'

Not just in England but in many countries all over the world the flame of the church is waning, and once again we need a reformation. Not a political reformation of church and state, nor one that is primarily of church practice, but a reformation in the hearts of believers that reignites the fire of love that should characterize the lives of Christians of all denominations. As the church increasingly fails to impact society, we are being forced to question the way we live out our corporate faith. If the changes that we must make to the way we 'do church' are to be more than merely a coat of paint on the relics of outdated tradition, they will have to be inspired by the reformed hearts of individuals who are seeking God beyond the framework of their church culture and experience.

If the church in the West is to survive as anything more than a marginalized, irrelevant, old institution we need to renew the covenant of love and grace that we once made with the Father. We must purge the church and our lives of idols and learn to live in the love and obedience that come from acknowledging God as God. When the bride of Christ renews her marriage vows, when his people return to him with faithful hearts, we will find that the dissonant clang that our religious clichés once made in the world will give way to a clear and unequivocal message of the hope that is to be found through faith in God. We cannot presume on God's patience and hide his light under a shroud of Christian culture and tradition for ever. The time to seek God with all of our hearts and minds and souls is now.

We may feel as if the foundations of our faith and church culture have been shaken, but God also appears to be shaking the very foundations of our society and exposing the idols in which the world has put its trust. When terrorists destroyed New York's Twin Towers in September 2001, most of us felt as if, in that one moment, the world had changed. The towers represented many of the things that our contemporary society looks to for hope and security, and in a devastating display of evil they were reduced to rubble in a matter of minutes. This was a humbling experience that revealed the fragility of our existence and no doubt many, even world leaders, called out to God that day. It will be interesting to see whether in the long term the result is a greater hunger for God, or whether our ability to recover from something as destructive as this so quickly will harden our hearts and strengthen our pride in our own self-sufficiency.

For many, though, faith is back on their personal agenda. As people become increasingly aware of just how thin the ice of our good-time culture really is, the search is on for something deeper. They are reflecting once again on spiritual values and looking for something more robust than the economy to put their trust in. Acts of terror and war have cast long shadows over our lives, and dark clouds of fear and uncertainty have gathered over a society that seems to have lost its way – a society that now more than ever needs a role model and a light set on a hill.

The events of 9/11 and subsequent acts of terror should be a wake-up call to all of us, a warning that things can change very quickly. The church has a new and exciting window of opportunity to rediscover her love for God and become a light in the darkness through the love, hope and peace she can bring to a frightened world – but it is a window that could close at any time. World leaders and politicians have some very difficult choices to make with regard to the role and freedom of religion in society, decisions that could have a long-term impact on the freedom the church currently enjoys. It calls for great wisdom from Christian leaders concerning how they behave in a society that increasingly and justifiably fears religion – and it reflects the tremendous wisdom of God when he declared that his people should be known primarily for their love.

When the temple in Jerusalem was destroyed some forty years after the crucifixion of Christ, it was a cataclysmic event for the people of Israel that sent a shockwave to Jews throughout the Roman Empire and beyond. Through its ruin, they lost an icon that was absolutely central to their beliefs. For the early church, though, it only confirmed what they already knew – that through the death of Christ, the temple, the place of worship and fellowship with God, had been relocated to the hearts of his people. When we learn to encounter God in the sanctuary of our hearts, when we restore this place of communion with him in our lives, those in the church will not fear as the symbols of modern society fall – and those in the world will see something in the church that offers greater security than the things in which they currently place their hope.

The temple destroyed by the Romans in AD70 was the third temple to be built on the same site in Jerusalem. It had been constructed by King Herod, replacing one built some five hundred years before, when the Jews returned to their homeland after a long exile in Babylon. The original temple, built by King Solomon, had been razed to the ground by the Babylonians during their conquest of Israel. Initial attempts by returning exiles to reconstruct the temple were met with fierce opposition. Eventually, as the people became discouraged, disappointed and fearful, they ceased building work for around eighteen years and gradually drifted into unfaithfulness.

The prophet Haggai recounts how God used drought, famine and poverty to refocus his people's attention on rebuilding his temple and how, as they heeded his discipline, God began to bless them.[4] The building work had only just started, and they had probably done little more than clear aside some of the rubble and lay a few stones, but the drought came to an end, and the following year, for the first time in many years, they could look forward to a decent harvest. They were a disappointed and broken people, a people crushed by seventy years of exile and demoralized by oppression at the hands of those who occupied their land. But it was these broken people that God chose to rebuild his temple.

We may have been exiled to the fringes of our church, and the church may find herself banished to the margins of society. We may have given up in discouragement and fear and resigned ourselves to the ruins of our faith. But it is the broken, crushed and marginalized stones that will provide a foundation for the church of the twenty-first century. When those at the fringe begin to seek God again, when we start to reform our personal faith and re-establish the temple of God in our hearts, we will find the blessing we have been longing for. All he requires is that we begin to place one stone on top of another, that we set our course to follow Christ and resume our spiritual journey – placing one faltering foot in front of the other, one step at a time.

> *"'Now give careful thought to this from this day on – consider how things were before one stone was laid on another in the LORD's temple. When anyone came to a heap of twenty measures, there were only ten. When anyone went to a wine vat to draw fifty measures, there were only twenty. I struck all the work of your hands with blight, mildew and hail, yet you did not turn to me,' declares the LORD. 'From this day on, from this twenty-fourth day of the ninth month, give careful thought to the day when the foundation of the LORD's temple was laid. Give careful thought: Is there yet any seed left in the barn? Until now, the vine and the fig-tree, the pomegranate and the olive tree have not borne fruit. From this day on I will bless you.'"*

Haggai 2:15-19

> *"For I know the plans I have for you," declares the LORD, "plans to prosper you and not to harm you, plans to give you hope and a future. Then you will call upon me and come and pray to me, and I will listen to you. You will seek me and find me when you seek me with all your heart. I will be found by*

you," declares the LORD, "and will bring you back from cap-
tivity. I will gather you from all the nations and places where
I have banished you," declares the LORD, "and will bring you
back to the place from which I carried you into exile."

Jeremiah 29:11-14

Beyond the fringe

It may seem as if the church has progressed a long way
in the half-millennium that has passed since the
Reformation, but has it really? Although we can define
the issues tackled by the reformers in terms of doctrines
and church practices, it could be argued that these were
just the products of human nature, that the roots of the
problem were really things like hunger for power, greed,
lovelessness and other types of worldliness that had
been assimilated into church culture over the preceding
centuries. If we take an honest look at our contemporary
church culture we might find that subtle forms of some
pre-Reformation practices have crept back in – and perhaps discover that in spite of changes in liturgy and
teaching, some were never really eradicated in the first
place.

The Reformation expressed itself in different ways
across Europe according to the prevailing leadership
and political circumstances. There were, however, a
number of key principles shared by most reformers. In
our search for a new experience of God and for fresh
ways of expressing our corporate faith, it is worth examining some of these principles – principles that may have
been lost as the church has reinvented itself over the
generations since the Reformation but which once
roused levels of commitment and passion that people
were willing to die for.

The chief objection of the reformers was the monopoly that the institution of the church held on God. Church leaders controlled the language of the Bible and excluded almost everybody apart from the clergy from access to Scripture. They defined sin and decided who could be forgiven and under what conditions. They decreed God's will and made people accountable to the church rather than to Christ. They portrayed God's image in a way that suited their own ends and deprived people of an understanding of the nature of Jesus. They robbed God of his magnificence, mystery and splendour and replaced it with the might of the church. God was placed in a carefully controlled box that underpinned the purposes of church leaders – and as a result, ordinary people were robbed of the possibility of a personal relationship with him.

The influences on today's church are not the same as in the middle ages: society is much more individualistic; people are better educated and much more scientifically and politically aware. Consequently the worldliness that has seeped into contemporary church culture is much less black and white. The Bible may be available in our mother tongue, but do we read and study it on our own or do we instead leave our faith in the hands of the church by allowing worship bands and celebrity preachers to replace our individual search for God? Do we dedicate time to developing a personal knowledge of God and an independent understanding of his teachings, or do we rely on the pre-packed version from our pulpits because the image of God projected by our church culture is more compatible with our lifestyles? Have we made grace superfluous by allowing political correctness to redefine sin, by abolishing accountability and replacing the law of love with a confusing cocktail of liberalism, law and conscience-calming Christian service?

Have we exchanged the mystery and wonder of God for evangelical clichés, unwittingly confining God to the box of church culture and robbing ourselves of a genuine personal relationship with him?

Disappointment and disillusionment with the church were a common bond that united the reformers. Many suffered rejection, betrayal, imprisonment and even horrific deaths – they knew about life at the fringe. But because they allowed their frustrations and hurts to initiate an intense search for a private and personal knowledge of God, they found something that reformed their hearts and lit a fire of reformation throughout the 'Christian' world. When we start to seek God independently, when we open our hearts to the love of God, when we allow his mystery and wonder to thrill our minds, we will initiate that process of reformation in our own lives – and those who are disappointed and broken at the fringe will light a flame that will bring life-giving reform to the ailing body of the church.

To the point

- If you examine your heart and the fruits of your labours, do you see evidence of God's blessing?
- Are there indications of his discipline?
- To what extent does what you do in church, your practices as part of a 'normal' Christian life and the principles you hold dear, reflect the nature and mission of Christ?
- Are you prepared to bring your hurts, disappointments and anger, no matter how justified they might be, and leave them at the feet of Christ?
- If you were to use the love of God as the acid test to assess 'worldliness' in your life and in the life of your

church, would there be areas of your life that you would seek to reform?

- When was the last time you read the Bible for pleasure?
- When was the last time you searched the scriptures for answers to the questions raised by your experience of life or church?
- If you felt God calling you to some form of greater commitment to him, what would you most fear to give up?
- Have you thought about the things you stand to gain by seeking God in a new way – without the straight-jacket of your negative experiences and the constraints of a faith driven mainly by church culture?

Meditation

The parable of the two sons

> *"What do you think? There was a man who had two sons. He went to the first and said, 'Son, go and work today in the vineyard.'*
>
> *"'I will not,' he answered, but later he changed his mind and went.*
>
> *"Then the father went to his other son and said the same thing. He answered, 'I will, sir,' but he did not go.*
>
> *"Which of the two did what his father wanted?"*
>
> *"The first," they answered.*
>
> Jesus said to them, "I tell you the truth, the tax collectors and the prostitutes are entering the kingdom of God ahead of you. For John came to you to show you the way of righteousness, and you did not believe him, but the tax collectors and the prostitutes did. And even after you saw this, you did not repent and believe him."

Matthew 21:28-32

- It is much easier to agree to follow Christ than it is to actually follow him.
- If we have drifted to the fringes of our churches or walked out on them altogether, it is not too late to change our minds and our hearts and go to work in the vineyard.
- If we pay lip-service to the Father's commands but then ignore them, we could end up like the scribes and Pharisees during the time of Christ – oblivious to their need of God and blind to his presence in their community.
- During his life on earth Jesus identified particularly with those at the fringes of society. We might feel like outcasts at the fringes of our churches, but if our response to Jesus is the same as that of the people he identified most with during his life, we may be among the first to find the blessings he promises.

Therefore, brothers, since we have confidence to enter the Most Holy Place by the blood of Jesus, by a new and living way opened for us through the curtain, that is, his body, and since we have a great priest over the house of God, let us draw near to God with a sincere heart in full assurance of faith, having our hearts sprinkled to cleanse us from a guilty conscience and having our bodies washed with pure water. Let us hold unswervingly to the hope we profess, for he who promised is faithful. And let us consider how we may spur one another on towards love and good deeds. Let us not give up meeting together, as some are in the habit of doing, but let us encourage one another – and all the more as you see the Day approaching.

Hebrews 10:19-25

"You say, 'I am rich; I have acquired wealth and do not need a thing.' But you do not realize that you are wretched, pitiful,

poor, blind and naked. I counsel you to buy from me gold refined in the fire, so that you can become rich; and white clothes to wear, so that you can cover your shameful nakedness; and salve to put on your eyes, so that you can see.

"Those whom I love I rebuke and discipline. So be earnest, and repent. Here I am! I stand at the door and knock. If anyone hears my voice and opens the door, I will come in and eat with him, and he with me."

Revelation 3:17-20

Prayer

Father, open my eyes to the true state of my heart and help me to hear clearly the message you are speaking to me. In your mercy, do not withdraw your discipline until my heart has been reformed by love and grace. Lead me, Lord, to repentance and a new revelation of your love for me, for your church and for your world. Let that love burn in my heart and shine out in my community. Amen.

Notes

[1] Ps. 73:21-22.
[2] 1 Kgs. 17:1.
[3] Heb. 12:5-11.
[4] Hag. 2:15-19.

Thanks

Just occasionally there is something nice about being proved wrong. Although in my disappointment and frustration I have often felt like writing the church off as the very last place we might find God, and despite the lovelessness I have at times witnessed, I must also admit that I have encountered many people in whom the love of Christ can truly be seen. At no time has this been more obvious than over the last couple of years as I have struggled to sort out my own spiritual journey – and in particular as I have tried to record those experiences in this book. I was warned that turning a raw manuscript into a publishable document would be the closest I could come, as a man, to having a baby. This has proved true in many ways but I doubt that many mothers have had quite as many helpers in the delivery ward as I have.

There are so many people to thank, not least our church family and house group in Didcot who have helped to carry our baggage for the most recent part of our journey – in particular Keith, a man of God with a true shepherd's heart who quietly and patiently brought 'church' to me at the fringe. But special thanks are also due to Jenny, Jonathan, Hazel, Dave and George, who read the manuscript at various stages and encouraged me to finish it. I also owe a big debt of thanks to Phil, who didn't bat an eyelid at my spelling and grammar when she proof-read the manuscript, and to David for writing the foreword. I feel tremendously blessed to have role models like David and Keith, both of whom have a unique gift of helping people to recognize their own value and significance. I am also extremely grateful to those who – named, renamed and unnamed – allowed me to use their stories as illustrations, especially to Sister Frances at Helen and Douglas House Hospice.

Confidence is something most of us struggle with, and I am grateful to Russ, who was probably the first person to tell me I could write (and because he is a professor I had to believe him), and also to friends and colleagues like Philip, Juan and others whose faith in my ability with words has helped give me the confidence to embark on this book. Confidence was also something that the team at Authentic Media were able to instil in me as I stepped into the strange world of Christian books. Their helpful input during the final stages of the manuscript and the professionalism with which Charlotte guided it through the publication process deserve a special mention.

I would like to thank my family: my parents, who shared some of the painful incidents recounted in the book as well as the pain of reading an early manuscript – and who also taught me to question and gave me the biblical framework for seeking answers; Diane and Mike, whose solid advice reflects the firm anchor they have always offered our somewhat nomadic family; my family in Germany and Canada, without whose support and encouragement I might never have finished the manuscript, and Christine, who always stood by us at the fringe. My biggest thanks, though, have to go to my wife Gabi and my children Natalie and Daniel, for whom my love has grown deeper and deeper as they have shared this journey with me.

Finally I would like to mention my grandmother, who saw a short item I had written on pain and who has nagged me about writing a book ever since. She may be nearly a hundred and frustrated by her frailty, but she knows what she wants and usually gets it. I hope she can see now how important her faithful prayers are for her children, grandchildren and great-grandchildren.